Book 1

The 96Th Academy Awards

The Stories Behind the Films, Actors, Directors, Artists, Actresses, And All that Nominated For The Show.

By

Paul N. Roy

Disclaimer

This book is intended for informational and entertainment purposes and should not be considered a substitute for professional advice.

Table of Contents

5

Introduction

This book isn't just a souvenir of the 96th Academy Awards; it's a backstage pass to the journeys that led these artists and their creations to Hollywood's grandest stage. We delve into the heart of each nominated film, unveiling the struggles, triumphs, and creative magic that brought them to life.

Meet the visionary directors who defied expectations with a groundbreaking narrative, the veteran actors who delivered a career-defining performance, and the fresh-faced talents who burst onto the scene with undeniable charisma. Each nominee, whether they graced the podium or not, has a story worth telling.

We'll travel alongside the resilient filmmakers who poured their heart into a personal project, the audacious screenwriters who challenged societal norms, and the fearless composers whose score resonated with audiences on a visceral level. These are the unsung heroes who contribute to the magic on screen.

But this book isn't just about individual triumphs. It's a tapestry woven from the year's most captivating narratives. We'll explore the themes that gripped audiences, the social issues that sparked conversation, and the artistic trends that pushed boundaries.

And, of course, we'll crown the champions. We'll celebrate the actors who captivated hearts and inhabited their roles with such depth they blurred the lines between fiction and reality. We'll applaud the directors who masterfully orchestrated their creative visions into cinematic symphonies. We'll raise a glass to the screenwriters who penned stories that transported us, challenged us, and made us laugh, cry, and everything in between.

So, step into the spotlight with us and turn the page. Let the 96th Academy Awards unfold, not just as a night of accolades, but as a testament to the enduring power of storytelling, the relentless pursuit of artistic excellence, and the unforgettable journeys that lead to Hollywood's biggest night. This book is your invitation to the after-party, where the stories behind the lights truly come alive.

Best Director

Justine Triet, "Anatomy of a Fall"

Justine Triet has carved her name into Oscar history, becoming only the third woman ever nominated for Best Director for her captivating courtroom drama, "Anatomy of a Fall." This nomination is a well-deserved recognition of her masterful storytelling, nuanced character development, and ability to craft a film that lingers long after the credits roll.

Triet's direction in "Anatomy of a Fall" is characterized by its precision and elegance. She creates a visually stunning world that subtly reflects the emotional complexities of the narrative. The stark, snow-covered landscapes of the French Alps mirror the coldness and isolation felt by the characters, while the claustrophobic interiors of the courtroom heighten the tension and drama.

But Triet's brilliance goes beyond aesthetics. Her camera lingers on subtle expressions and silent exchanges, allowing the audience to decipher the unspoken truths and hidden emotions beneath the surface. She deftly handles the film's complex pacing, alternating between intense courtroom confrontations and quieter moments of introspection, keeping the viewer engaged and emotionally invested throughout.

Triet's ability to elicit powerful performances from her actors is another hallmark of her directorial skill. Sandra Hüller delivers a captivating performance as the enigmatic Franziska Janus, while Lars Eidinger shines as her cunning defense attorney. Triet seamlessly navigates the ensemble cast, ensuring each character, regardless of their screen time, contributes meaningfully to the narrative tapestry.

More than just a gripping courtroom drama, "Anatomy of a Fall" delves into the intricacies of human relationships, exploring themes of love, loss, betrayal, and the ambiguity of truth. Triet masterfully dissects the dynamics of the central couple, leaving the audience questioning their motivations and culpability until the very end.

Triet's nomination is not just a personal triumph; it's a victory for female filmmakers everywhere. Her inclusion in the Best Director category signifies a positive shift in the industry, one that recognizes the unique perspectives and storytelling talents of women directors.

With "Anatomy of a Fall," Justine Triet has established herself as a force to be reckoned with. Her masterful direction, insightful storytelling, and ability to captivate audiences with complex characters and a thought-provoking narrative make her a deserving nominee for the coveted Best Director award. And with her groundbreaking presence in this category, she inspires the next generation of female filmmakers to dream big and reach for the highest accolades.

Martin Scorsese, "Killers of the Flower Moon"

Martin Scorsese, a name synonymous with cinematic excellence, has once again woven his magic with "Killers of the Flower Moon," earning a well-deserved 2024 Oscar nomination for Best

Director. This haunting historical drama transports viewers to the heart of 1920s Oklahoma, where the idyllic life of the Osage Nation is shattered by a string of deadly attacks. Scorsese's masterful direction crafts a visually stunning and emotionally resonant film, solidifying his position as a cinematic giant.

Scorsese paints a vivid portrait of the Osage Nation before the oil boom, capturing their rich culture and traditions with sensitivity and respect. Lush landscapes bathed in warm sunlight evoke a sense of tranquility, a stark contrast to the darkness that soon engulfs the community. As violence descends, Scorsese masterfully builds suspense, utilizing shadows and stark close-ups to convey the growing fear and paranoia.

Beyond the visual mastery, Scorsese excels in bringing his characters to life. Leonardo DiCaprio delivers a nuanced performance as FBI agent Ernest Burkhart, torn between his duty to uphold the law and his growing empathy for the Osage people.

Lily Gladstone shines as Mollie Kyle, a woman fueled by grief and unwavering determination to seek justice for her murdered sister. Scorsese orchestrates powerful scenes between these and other characters, showcasing the human cost of corruption and the enduring spirit of those fighting for justice.

"Killers of the Flower Moon" is not just a historical drama; it's a poignant commentary on greed, power, and the fight for Indigenous rights. Scorsese doesn't shy away from the brutal realities of the era, yet he balances it with moments of tenderness and resilience. His direction amplifies the film's emotional core, leaving audiences heartbroken by the injustices faced by the Osage people and inspired by their unwavering spirit.

Scorsese's nomination for Best Director is a testament to his enduring talent and his ability to tell important stories with exceptional skill. In "Killers of the Flower Moon," he has crafted a film that is both visually stunning and emotionally impactful, ensuring its place among his cinematic masterpieces.

This nomination is not just a personal recognition, but a celebration of filmmaking that shines a light on historical injustices and celebrates the human spirit in the face of adversity.

Christopher Nolan, "Oppenheimer"

Christopher Nolan, a visionary filmmaker known for his mind-bending narratives and technical prowess, has earned yet another well-deserved Oscar nomination – this time for Best Director with his epic biopic "Oppenheimer." The film delves into the life and work of J. Robert Oppenheimer, the "father of the atomic bomb," offering a breathtakingly immersive and emotionally charged exploration of ambition, responsibility, and the consequences of scientific progress.

Nolan's direction in "Oppenheimer" is nothing short of masterful. He employs his signature IMAX format to create a visually stunning spectacle, placing the audience at the heart of the Manhattan Project and the Trinity test, the first detonation of an atomic bomb. The sheer scale and power of these sequences are awe-inspiring, leaving a lasting impression on the viewer.

But beyond the visual spectacle, Nolan excels in capturing the emotional complexities of his characters. Cillian Murphy delivers a transformative performance as Oppenheimer, a man grappling with the weight of his creation and the potential for its destruction. Nolan navigates the character's internal struggles with nuance and depth, allowing the audience to empathize with Oppenheimer's ambition while also questioning its ultimate cost.

The film's pacing is masterfully controlled, building tension and suspense as it explores the ethical and political machinations behind the development of the atomic bomb. Nolan expertly weaves archival footage and newsreels into the narrative, seamlessly blending historical fact with dramatic fiction to create a powerful and immersive experience.

"Oppenheimer" is not merely a biopic; it's a meditation on the potential of science and the responsibility that comes with it. Nolan doesn't shy away from the moral ambiguity surrounding the creation of the atomic bomb, forcing the audience to grapple with difficult questions about human ambition and the price of progress.

His nomination for Best Director is a testament to his ability to craft a film that is both technically dazzling and emotionally resonant. In "Oppenheimer," Nolan has created a visually stunning and thought-provoking masterpiece, solidifying his position as a true visionary filmmaker. This nomination is not just a personal recognition, but a celebration of his ability to take audiences on unforgettable journeys that challenge our understanding of the world and ourselves.

Yorgos Lanthimos, "Poor Things"

With his latest film, "Poor Things," Yorgos Lanthimos has once again proven his mastery of the bizarre and grotesque, earning a well-deserved 2024 Oscar nomination for Best Director.

This darkly comedic Victorian fantasy revolves around Bella Baxter, a reanimated woman with the brain of a child, and explores themes of identity, love, and the complexities of human nature with his signature absurdist humor and unsettling brilliance.

Lanthimos crafts a visually stunning world in "Poor Things," drawing inspiration from Victorian paintings and literature while injecting his own unique aesthetic. The opulent costumes and meticulous set design juxtapose seamlessly with the film's dark humor and unconventional characters, creating a world that is both familiar and deeply strange.

But Lanthimos' brilliance lies beyond aesthetics. He masterfully navigates the tonal shifts between whimsical comedy and unsettling drama, keeping the audience engaged and surprised throughout. His direction of actors is impeccable, drawing out nuanced performances from Emma Stone as the innocent and playful Bella Baxter and Mark Ruffalo as the eccentric scientist who created her.

The film delves into complex themes of human connection and empathy, challenging societal norms and expectations. Lanthimos uses Bella's childlike perspective to highlight the absurdity of social constructs and the hypocrisy of Victorian morality. He masterfully blends humor and pathos, forcing us to confront uncomfortable truths about ourselves and the world we live in.

More than just a director, Lanthimos is a true auteur, shaping every aspect of his films from the script to the score. His unique voice and uncompromising vision are evident in every frame of "Poor Things," making it a truly singular cinematic experience.

His nomination for Best Director is a significant recognition of his talent and his contribution to the world of cinema. In "Poor Things," Lanthimos has crafted a film that is both entertaining and thought-provoking, challenging audiences to see the world through a new lens and question the very nature of existence. This nomination signifies not just a personal triumph, but a validation of his unique cinematic vision and a testament to his ability to push the boundaries of storytelling.

Jonathan Glazer, "The Zone of Interest"

Jonathan Glazer, known for his visually striking and emotionally complex films, takes a minimalist approach in "The Zone of Interest," earning him a well-deserved 2024 Oscar nomination for Best Director. This chilling adaptation of Martin Amis' novel explores the daily lives of an Auschwitz commandant and his family living mere steps from the horrors within the camp. Glazer's masterful direction utilizes silence and subtle nuances to create a film that is both haunting and thought-provoking.

Glazer eschews the typical visual depictions of violence associated with Holocaust narratives. Instead, he focuses on the unsettling proximity of evil, placing the audience within the idyllic home of the Höss family, mere footsteps from the gas chambers. The camera lingers on everyday moments, a child's laughter, a family dinner, creating a stark contrast to the unimaginable suffering just beyond their walls.

This juxtaposition makes the film all the more unsettling, forcing us to confront the banality of evil and the ease with which it can become normalized.

The performances, expertly guided by Glazer, are mesmerizing in their restraint. Christian Friedel portrays Rudolf Höss, the Auschwitz commandant, with a chilling detachment, his eyes betraying a flicker of unease amidst a mask of indifference. Sandra Hüller as his wife, Hedwig, embodies a mix of naiveté and willful ignorance, highlighting the complexities of complicity. Glazer draws remarkable performances from his cast, even with minimal dialogue, relying on subtle shifts in expression and gesture to convey the characters' inner turmoil.

The soundscape of "The Zone of Interest" plays a crucial role in Glazer's vision. The film is filled with an ambient soundscape of distant sirens, muffled screams, and the ever-present hum of the camp's machinery. These sounds, although not explicit depictions of violence, create a constant sense of dread and unease, forcing the audience to confront the horrors unfolding just beyond the frame.

Glazer's nomination for Best Director is a testament to his ability to create a film that is both visually stunning and emotionally harrowing. In "The Zone of Interest," he eschews melodrama and graphic depictions of violence, opting instead for a more nuanced and haunting approach. He forces us to confront the complexities of evil and the silence that allows it to flourish, making this film a powerful and

unforgettable cinematic experience.

Best Supporting Actor

Sterling K. Brown, "American Fiction"

Sterling K. Brown, the celebrated actor known for his captivating performances in "This Is Us" and "Black Panther," has garnered yet another prestigious accolade with his nomination for Best Supporting Actor at the 2024 Oscar awards. This time, the spotlight shines on his powerful portrayal in the critically acclaimed film "American Fiction."

Written and directed by Cord Jefferson, "American Fiction" is a poignant satire that delves into the complexities of race and representation in the literary world. The film follows Thelonious "Monk" Ellison (played by Jeffrey Wright), a disillusioned novelist who, in a bold act of protest, writes a stereotypical "Black" novel under a pseudonym.

The book unexpectedly becomes a runaway success, catapulting Monk and his family, including his brother Clifford (played by Brown), into the heart of a cultural maelstrom.

Brown delivers a nuanced and multifaceted performance as Clifford, a successful surgeon navigating the tensions between his personal and professional life. He embodies the character's frustration with his brother's choices while offering unwavering support, showcasing the intricate dynamics of familial bonds. Critics have lauded Brown's portrayal, praising his ability to navigate the emotional spectrum with depth and sensitivity.

This nomination comes as no surprise to those who have followed Brown's meteoric rise. He has consistently delivered captivating performances, earning an Emmy Award for his role in "This Is Us" and critical acclaim for his work in films like "Black Panther" and "Waves." Brown's talent lies in his ability to inhabit diverse characters with authenticity and vulnerability, captivating audiences across genres.

The nomination for "American Fiction" further solidifies Brown's position as a force to be reckoned with in Hollywood. It not only recognizes his exceptional talent but also highlights the importance of diverse storytelling and the need for nuanced portrayals of Black characters in mainstream media. As the awards ceremony approaches, the anticipation builds to see if Brown will take home the coveted golden statuette, adding another chapter to his remarkable career.

Whether he wins or not, Brown's performance in "American Fiction" has already left a lasting impression. His nomination serves as a testament to his dedication to his craft and his ability to elevate storytelling with his powerful presence.

Robert De Niro, "Killers of the Flower Moon"

Robert De Niro, the legendary actor with a career spanning decades and countless iconic roles, has once again garnered critical acclaim and awards recognition for his performance in Martin Scorsese's historical drama "Killers of the Flower Moon." De Niro's portrayal of the sinister William Hale in the film has earned him a well-deserved nomination for Best Supporting Actor at the 2024 Academy Awards.

Based on David Grann's acclaimed book of the same name, "Killers of the Flower Moon" tells the true story of a series of murders that plagued the Osage Nation in the 1920s, following the discovery of oil on their land. De Niro steps into the shoes of Hale, a ruthless cattleman and ranch owner who becomes deeply involved in the conspiracy to exploit the Osage people and seize their wealth.

De Niro delivers a chilling and nuanced performance as Hale, perfectly capturing the character's quiet menace and calculating nature.

He avoids overplaying the villainy, instead opting for a portrayal that is all the more unsettling for its understated evil. His steely gaze and measured delivery convey a sense of unwavering determination and a complete lack of remorse for his actions.

Critics have praised De Niro's performance, highlighting his ability to imbue Hale with a sense of chilling authenticity. Peter Bradshaw of The Guardian called it "a masterfully controlled performance," while David Rooney of The Hollywood Reporter wrote that De Niro "gives us a portrait of a man whose outward respectability masks a heart as black as oil."

De Niro's nomination for "Killers of the Flower Moon" is a testament to his enduring talent and his ability to consistently deliver captivating performances. It adds to his already impressive collection of accolades, which includes two Academy Awards, a Golden Globe Award, and a BAFTA Award.

Whether he takes home the golden statuette or not, De Niro's performance in "Killers of the Flower Moon" is sure to be remembered as one of his finest. It is a chilling portrayal of a complex and morally reprehensible character, and a reminder of the enduring power of his acting talents.

Robert Downey Jr., "Oppenheimer"

Robert Downey Jr., the Hollywood icon synonymous with his charismatic portrayal of Iron Man, has traded in his superhero suit for a complex and nuanced performance in Christopher Nolan's historical drama "Oppenheimer." His captivating portrayal of Lewis Strauss, the controversial chairman of the Atomic Energy Commission, has earned him a well-deserved nomination for Best Supporting Actor at the 2024 Academy Awards.

Set against the backdrop of World War II, "Oppenheimer" chronicles the development of the atomic bomb and the moral complexities surrounding its creation.

Downey Jr. steps into the shoes of Strauss, a brilliant but morally ambiguous figure who played a pivotal role in the Manhattan Project.

Downey Jr. delivers a layered and thought-provoking performance as Strauss, grappling with the immense responsibility and ethical dilemmas associated with the atomic bomb. He avoids portraying Strauss as a one-dimensional villain, instead offering a nuanced portrayal of a man driven by ambition, patriotism, and a deep sense of duty. His portrayal is both captivating and unsettling, forcing audiences to confront the complexities of the character and the historical context surrounding him.

Critics have lauded Downey Jr.'s performance, praising his ability to imbue Strauss with a sense of gravitas and vulnerability. Owen Gleiberman of Variety wrote that Downey Jr. "gives a performance that's both shrewd and haunted," while Alonso Duralde of The Wrap called it "a master class in underplaying."

Downey Jr.'s nomination for "Oppenheimer" marks a significant departure from his recent superhero roles, showcasing his versatility and range as an actor. It adds to his already impressive collection of accolades, which includes two Golden Globe Awards and a BAFTA Award.

Whether he takes home the golden statuette or not, Downey Jr.'s performance in "Oppenheimer" is sure to be remembered as a turning point in his career. It is a captivating portrayal of a complex and morally ambiguous character, and a testament to his enduring talent and ability to consistently deliver powerful performances.

Downey Jr.'s nomination is particularly notable as it comes amidst a highly competitive awards season. He faces stiff competition from fellow nominees like Sterling K. Brown ("American Fiction") and Willem Dafoe ("The Northman"), but his nuanced and captivating performance stands out as a true force to be reckoned with.

The 96th Academy Awards ceremony will be held on March 3, 2024, where the winner of the Best Supporting Actor category will be announced. Regardless of the outcome, Downey Jr.'s performance in "Oppenheimer" is sure to leave a lasting impression on audiences and solidify his position as one of the most talented and versatile actors of his generation.

Ryan Gosling, "Barbie"

Ryan Gosling, the Canadian heartthrob known for his charming demeanor and captivating performances in films like "La La Land" and "Drive," has taken a bold step into the world of pink plastic and Mattel this year with his role in Greta Gerwig's highly anticipated live-action film "Barbie." His portrayal of the iconic Ken doll has not only garnered him critical acclaim but also a coveted nomination for Best Supporting Actor at the 2024 Academy Awards.

Barbie takes a subversive approach to the classic toy line, following Barbie (played by Margot Robbie) as she is unceremoniously ejected from Barbie Land for failing to conform to its unrealistic standards of perfection. Landing in the "real world," Barbie embarks on a journey of self-discovery, challenging societal expectations and redefining what it means to be a plastic fantastic role model.

Gosling's Ken, far from being the vacuous and perpetually tanned accessory viewers might expect, is portrayed as a surprisingly complex and layered character. He is a loyal and supportive partner to Barbie, but also harbors his own insecurities and anxieties about masculinity and his place in the world.

Gosling delivers a delightful and nuanced performance, balancing Ken's inherent absurdity with a genuine sweetness and vulnerability. He infuses the character with physical humor and comedic timing, perfectly capturing the awkward charm of a man who is literally made of plastic. Critics have praised his performance, calling it "hilarious" and "surprisingly touching."

The nomination for "Barbie" marks a significant departure from Gosling's usual dramatic roles, showcasing his comedic talents and willingness to take on risks. It adds to his already impressive collection of accolades, which includes two Golden Globe nominations and an Independent Spirit Award.

Whether he takes home the golden statuette or not, Gosling's performance in "Barbie" is sure to be remembered as one of his most memorable. It is a delightful and nuanced portrayal of an iconic character, and a testament to his enduring talent and comedic prowess.

Gosling's nomination is particularly noteworthy as it comes in a year where the Best Supporting Actor category is fiercely competitive. He faces stiff competition from fellow nominees like Sterling K. Brown ("American Fiction") and Robert Downey Jr. ("Oppenheimer"), but his unique and captivating performance stands out as a true force to be reckoned with.

Mark Ruffalo, "Poor Things"

Mark Ruffalo, the acclaimed actor known for his captivating performances in both blockbuster franchises like "The Avengers" and critically acclaimed dramas like "Spotlight," has garnered yet another prestigious accolade with his nomination for Best Supporting Actor at the 2024 Oscar awards. This time, the spotlight shines on his nuanced portrayal in Yorgos Lanthimos' darkly comedic and thought-provoking film, "Poor Things."

Set in Victorian England, "Poor Things" tells the story of Belle Baxter (Emma Stone), a beautiful young woman who has been brought back to life using unconventional methods. Navigating the complexities of society and her own newfound sentience, Belle finds herself entangled in a web of love, loss, and revenge. Ruffalo steps into the shoes of Dr. Godwin Baxter, Belle's eccentric creator and a scientist obsessed with pushing the boundaries of life and death.

Critics have lauded Ruffalo's performance, praising his ability to bring depth and complexity to a character that could easily have fallen into caricature. Peter Debruge of Variety writes, "Ruffalo delivers a performance that is equal parts charming and unsettling, perfectly capturing the character's manic energy and underlying moral ambiguity." David Ehrlich of IndieWire adds, "Ruffalo steals the show with a performance that is both hilarious and heartbreaking, reminding us once again of his immense talent and range."

Ruffalo's nomination comes as no surprise to those who have followed his impressive career. He has consistently delivered compelling performances, earning an Emmy Award for his role in "The Normal Heart" and numerous accolades for his work in films like "Zodiac" and "Foxcatcher." His ability to seamlessly transition between genres and inhabit diverse characters showcases his versatility and dedication to his craft.

The nomination for "Poor Things" further solidifies Ruffalo's position as a force to be reckoned with in Hollywood. It not only recognizes his exceptional talent but also highlights the power of his performance in elevating the film's exploration of themes like mortality, identity, and the very nature of humanity. As the awards ceremony approaches, the anticipation builds to see if Ruffalo will take home the coveted golden statuette, adding another chapter to his remarkable career.

Whether he wins or not, Ruffalo's performance in "Poor Things" has already left a lasting impression. It is a nuanced and captivating portrayal of a complex character, and a testament to his enduring talent and ability to consistently deliver powerful performances.

Best Costume Design

"Barbie" – Jacqueline Durran

The whimsical and vibrant world of Barbie has come to life on the big screen in Greta Gerwig's critically acclaimed live-action film, and a major part of its success is due to the dazzling and imaginative costume design by Jacqueline Durran. Her work in "Barbie" has earned her a well-deserved nomination for Best Costume Design at the 2024 Academy Awards.

Durran, a two-time Oscar winner for her work on "Little Women" and "Anna Karenina," has masterfully translated the iconic Barbie aesthetic into a cinematic reality. Her costumes are not just visually stunning, but also serve as integral character portrayals, reflecting the personalities and journeys of the characters within the film.

For Margot Robbie's Barbie, Durran created a wardrobe that is both playful and empowering. From her hot pink power suit to her whimsical mermaid gown, each outfit embodies Barbie's signature style while also hinting at her inner strength and determination.

Ryan Gosling's Ken, on the other hand, is portrayed through a more muted and pastel color palette, reflecting his initial naivety and conformity to traditional gender norms. However, as Ken evolves throughout the film, his wardrobe becomes more daring and expressive, mirroring his newfound self-awareness.

The supporting characters in "Barbie" are also brought to life through their unique and eye-catching costumes. From the neon-drenched roller-skating gang to the pastel-clad inhabitants of Barbieland, each outfit contributes to the film's overall aesthetic and world-building.

Durran's use of color, texture, and silhouette is masterful throughout the film. She seamlessly blends high fashion references with playful nods to the original Barbie dolls, creating a visually stunning and cohesive world.

The nomination for "Barbie" is a testament to Durran's creativity, skill, and attention to detail. Her costumes are not just visually stunning, but they also play a vital role in storytelling and character development. Whether she takes home the golden statuette or not, Durran's work on "Barbie" is sure to leave a lasting impression on audiences and fellow costume designers alike.

In addition to her nomination for Best Costume Design, "Barbie" is also nominated for Best Production Design, making it a strong contender in the upcoming awards season. The film's playful and subversive take on the iconic toy line has resonated with audiences and critics alike, and it is sure to continue to be a topic of conversation for years to come.

"Killers of the Flower Moon" – Jacqueline West

Jacqueline West, the acclaimed costume designer known for her meticulous attention to historical detail, has garnered a well-deserved nomination for Best Costume Design at the 2024 Academy Awards for her work on Martin Scorsese's epic historical drama, "Killers of the Flower Moon."

Set in 1920s Oklahoma, the film tells the true story of the Osage Nation, a wealthy Native American tribe targeted by a series of brutal murders following the discovery of oil on their land. West's costumes play a crucial role in transporting viewers back to this specific time and place, while also serving to highlight the stark contrasts between the opulent lifestyles of the oil tycoons and the traditional dress of the Osage people.

West meticulously researched Osage culture and attire, collaborating closely with Osage consultant Julie O'Keefe to ensure the costumes were both historically accurate and culturally sensitive. She sourced vintage clothing and fabrics, and even worked with Osage artisans to create intricate beadwork and other traditional embellishments.

For the Osage characters, West created garments that reflected their cultural heritage and individual personalities. Molly (played by Lily Gladstone), for instance, is often seen wearing traditional Osage clothing, signifying her connection to her roots. Meanwhile, Ernest Burkhart (played by Jesse

Plemons), a young Osage man who has assimilated into white society, is dressed in more modern attire.

The film also portrays the opulent world of the oil tycoons, who flaunt their wealth through lavish clothing and accessories. West's costumes for these characters are in stark contrast to those of the Osage people, highlighting the economic and social disparities between the two groups.

For example, William Hale (played by Robert De Niro), a ruthless cattleman and oil baron, is often seen wearing expensive suits and Stetsons, symbolizing his power and privilege.

West's masterful use of costume design not only transports viewers to 1920s Oklahoma but also helps to tell the story of the film. The contrasting styles of dress worn by the Osage people and the oil tycoons visually represent the conflict and tension that lie at the heart of the narrative.

The nomination for Best Costume Design is a testament to West's talent and dedication to her craft. Her costumes are not just visually stunning, but they also play a vital role in enriching the story and characters of "Killers of the Flower Moon." Whether she takes home the golden statuette or not, West's work on the film is sure to leave a lasting impression on audiences and fellow costume designers alike.

In addition to her nomination for Best Costume Design, "Killers of the Flower Moon" has also received nine other Oscar nominations, including Best Picture, Best Director, and Best Actor for Leonardo DiCaprio. The film is a powerful and timely exploration of greed, corruption, and the fight for justice, and it is sure to be a major contender at the upcoming awards ceremony.

David Crossman, Janty Yates "Napoleon"

Costume designers David Crossman and Janty Yates brought the grandeur and intimacy of Napoleon Bonaparte's life to the big screen in Ridley Scott's historical epic "napoleon." Their collaborative effort resulted in a nomination for best costume design at the 2024 academy awards, a testament to their meticulous research, artistry, and ability to capture the essence of a bygone era.

Crossman, known for his expertise in military history, took on the responsibility of designing the film's vast array of military uniforms. He meticulously researched French military attire from the late 18th and early 19th centuries, ensuring historical accuracy while also infusing the costumes with a sense of drama and visual impact. The iconic bicorne hats, worn by Napoleon and his officers, were a particular focus, with Crossman creating multiple variations that reflected the character's evolving status and persona.

Yates, a seasoned costume designer with multiple academy award nominations to her name, focused on the civilian attire of the film's characters, particularly the opulent gowns and accessories worn by Napoleon's wife, josephine (played by vanessa kirby). yates' designs were inspired by the fashions of the directoire and empire periods, characterized by their elegance, neoclassical influences, and use of luxurious fabrics. She also created a distinct visual identity for Josephine, reflecting her personality and evolving relationship with napoleon.

The success of "Napoleon"'s costume design lies in the seamless blend of crossman and yates' individual strengths. Crossman's military expertise ensured historical accuracy, while yates' eye for detail and flair for the dramatic brought the characters to life. together, they created a visually stunning and historically evocative world that transported audiences back to the napoleonic era.

The nomination for best costume design is a well-deserved recognition of Crossman and yates' outstanding work on "napoleon." Their costumes are not only visually stunning but also play a crucial role in shaping the film's narrative and immersing viewers in its world.

Ellen Mirojnick- "Oppenheimer"

Seasoned costume designer Ellen Mirojnick finally received her first Academy Award nomination for her meticulous work on Christopher Nolan's historical drama "Oppenheimer." The film, which chronicles the life and work of the "father of the atomic bomb," J. Robert Oppenheimer, presented a unique challenge for Mirojnick, requiring her to capture the essence of the 1940s and 50s while also reflecting the film's themes of scientific advancement, ethical dilemmas, and the weight of history.

Mirojnick's approach to costume design in "Oppenheimer" was one of meticulous research and attention to detail. She delved into historical photographs, film footage, and fashion archives to recreate the clothing styles of the period, ensuring authenticity in both military uniforms and civilian attire. For the scientists working on the Manhattan Project, she designed practical yet sophisticated garments that reflected their intelligence and dedication. For Oppenheimer himself, played by Cillian Murphy, she created a wardrobe that evolved throughout the film, subtly mirroring his internal struggles and the growing weight of his decisions.

While historical accuracy was paramount, Mirojnick also used costumes to enhance the film's narrative and visual storytelling. The stark contrast between the khaki uniforms of the military and the muted tones of the scientists' attire highlighted the different worlds they inhabited. The use of color, particularly in Oppenheimer's clothing, became increasingly muted as the film progressed, reflecting his growing disillusionment and the potential consequences of his work.

Mirojnick's nomination for Best Costume Design is a significant milestone in her long and successful career. It recognizes her ability to not only recreate a specific historical period but also use costume as a powerful tool to shape the film's emotional impact and thematic resonance. With "Oppenheimer," she has delivered a masterclass in costume design, creating a visually stunning and historically accurate world that serves the film's narrative and elevates its emotional core.

Ellen Mirojnick's work on "Oppenheimer" is a testament to the power of costume design in filmmaking. Her meticulous attention to detail, her ability to capture the essence of a historical era, and her use of costume as a storytelling tool have all contributed to the film's success and her well-deserved Academy Award nomination.

"Poor Things" – Holly Waddington

Holly Waddington, costume designer
Costume designer Holly Waddington's vibrant and imaginative creations for Yorgos Lanthimos' darkly comedic film "Poor Things" earned her a much-deserved nomination for Best Costume Design at the 2024 Academy Awards. The film, based on Alasdair Gray's novel of the same name, tells the fantastical story of a young woman brought back to life using unorthodox methods and her subsequent adventures across continents. Waddington's costumes played a crucial role in bringing this whimsical world to life, capturing the film's unique blend of historical setting, fantastical elements, and social commentary.

The film takes place in Victorian-era England, and Waddington meticulously researched the fashions of the period. However, she didn't simply replicate historical styles; she imbued them with her own playful touch, using bold colors, quirky patterns, and unexpected combinations to create a sense of whimsy and otherworldliness. For example, the protagonist, Belle Baxter (played by Emma Stone), is often seen wearing brightly colored dresses with unconventional silhouettes, reflecting her unconventional character and newfound freedom.

Waddington also used costumes to highlight the film's social commentary. Belle's clothing, for instance, becomes increasingly daring as she challenges societal norms and embraces her independence. In contrast, the more conservative characters are often dressed in muted tones and traditional styles, emphasizing their rigid adherence to societal expectations.

The film also features fantastical elements, most notably Belle's unique anatomy – she has the head of a beautiful young woman but the body of a Frankenstein's monster. Waddington designed a special prosthetic suit for this character, ensuring it was both visually striking and believable within the film's world. The suit also served as a metaphor for Belle's struggle to fit into society and reconcile her different parts.

Waddington's nomination for Best Costume Design is a testament to her creativity, skill, and understanding of the film's unique vision. Her costumes are not only visually stunning but also play a crucial role in shaping the film's narrative, characters, and thematic resonance. With "Poor Things," she has delivered a masterclass in costume design, creating a world that is both whimsical and thought-provoking.

Best Makeup And Hairstyling

"Golda"

The transformation of Helen Mirren into the iconic Israeli Prime Minister Golda Meir in Guy Nattiv's historical drama "Golda" was a triumph of makeup and hairstyling artistry. The team responsible for this remarkable feat, led by Karen Hartley Thomas (makeup designer), Suzi Battersby (prosthetics designer), and Ashra Kelly-Blue (prosthetic makeup artist), received a well-deserved nomination for Best Makeup and Hairstyling at the 2024 Academy Awards.

Meir's distinctive appearance, characterized by her strong features, expressive eyes, and signature bun hairstyle, posed a significant challenge for the makeup and hair team. Their meticulous attention to detail and skillful application of prosthetics and makeup not only achieved a remarkable physical resemblance but also captured the essence of Meir's personality and resilience.

To achieve the desired likeness, the team used a combination of advanced prosthetic techniques and makeup artistry. Battersby created custom-made facial prosthetics, including a nose bridge, eye bags, and a neckpiece, that subtly altered Mirren's features to match Meir's. Kelly-Blue then applied intricate makeup, paying close attention to Meir's skin tone, wrinkles, and age spots to further enhance the resemblance.

Hairstylist Hartley Thomas played a crucial role in completing the transformation. She meticulously replicated Meir's signature bun hairstyle, ensuring it was not only accurate but also conveyed the character's strength and authority.

The hairstyle, along with the makeup and prosthetics, became an integral part of Meir's on-screen persona, instantly recognizable to audiences familiar with the historical figure.

The makeup and hairstyling in "Golda" went beyond simply creating a physical likeness. The team also used these elements to subtly convey Meir's emotional state and the toll of leadership during a tumultuous period in Israeli history. Subtle changes in makeup, such as the use of darker tones under her eyes, hinted at fatigue and stress, while the hairstyle remained meticulously neat and composed, reflecting Meir's unwavering determination.

The nomination for Best Makeup and Hairstyling is a well-deserved recognition of the exceptional artistry and dedication of the team behind "Golda."

Their work not only contributed to the film's historical accuracy but also played a crucial role in bringing the character of Golda Meir to life on screen, capturing her physical essence, strength, and emotional depth.

"Maestro"

Maestro, the biographical drama about iconic composer Leonard Bernstein, not only captivated audiences with its powerful story but also garnered recognition for its exceptional makeup and hairstyling achievements. The talented team of Naomi Donne (makeup designer), Mike Marino (prosthetic makeup designer), and Shane Thomas (hair designer) received a well-deserved nomination for Best Makeup and Hairstyling at the 2024 Academy Awards, a testament to their artistry and transformative skills.

The film spans several decades of Bernstein's life, presenting a unique challenge for the makeup and hair team. They needed to seamlessly transition Bradley Cooper's appearance to capture the maestro's physical evolution throughout the years, while maintaining a striking resemblance to the real-life figure.

Donne and Marino employed a combination of makeup and prosthetics to achieve this remarkable transformation.

Custom-made facial prosthetics, including nose pieces, jowls, and age spots, were meticulously applied to subtly alter Cooper's facial features and reflect Bernstein's changing age. Donne then used her makeup artistry to further refine the resemblance, paying close attention to Bernstein's unique skin tone, wrinkles, and the telltale mole below his lip.

Hairstylist Shane Thomas played a crucial role in completing the transformation. He meticulously researched Bernstein's hairstyles throughout his life, ensuring each era was accurately portrayed.

From the youthful tousled locks of his early career to the iconic salt-and-pepper mane of his later years, Thomas meticulously recreated Bernstein's signature styles, using subtle changes in length, volume, and color to reflect the passage of time and Bernstein's evolving persona.

The makeup and hairstyling in "Maestro" went beyond simply creating a physical likeness.

Donne, Marino, and Thomas used these elements to subtly convey Bernstein's emotional state and the impact of his tumultuous life on his appearance. The gradual thinning of his hair and the deepening of wrinkles mirrored the weight of his career and personal struggles, while the carefully chosen hairstyles reflected his shifting moods and artistic phases.

The success of "Maestro"'s makeup and hairstyling lies in the seamless collaboration between Donne, Marino, and Thomas. Their deep understanding of Bernstein's life and character, combined with their technical expertise and artistic vision, resulted in a transformative and evocative portrayal that resonated with audiences and critics alike.

The nomination for Best Makeup and Hairstyling is a well-deserved recognition of the exceptional artistry and dedication of the team behind "Maestro." Their work not only contributed to the film's historical accuracy and emotional depth but also played a crucial role in bringing the iconic Leonard Bernstein to life on screen, capturing his essence and complexities with remarkable fidelity.

"Oppenheimer"

In the race for the 2024 Academy Award for Best Makeup and Hairstyling, Christopher Nolan's historical epic "Oppenheimer" stands out with its meticulously crafted transformations, earning a well-deserved spot among the nominees.

The film chronicles the life and work of J. Robert Oppenheimer, the "father of the atomic bomb," and the team behind the makeup and hairstyling, led by Christopher Allen Nelson (makeup designer), Shane Thomas (hair designer), and Julia Vernon (prosthetic makeup artist), masterfully navigated the complex task of aging the cast and transporting them to the specific periods depicted.

The film spans several decades, showcasing Oppenheimer's journey from a young, ambitious physicist to a man burdened by the consequences of his scientific achievements.

Nelson and Thomas employed a combination of subtle makeup techniques and intricate prosthetics to convincingly age the cast members while maintaining their individual facial structures.

Cillian Murphy, portraying Oppenheimer, underwent a particularly remarkable transformation, his youthful features gradually etched with lines of worry and fatigue as the film progresses.

Vernon's expertise in prosthetic makeup played a crucial role in achieving historical accuracy. For instance, prosthetics were used to replicate the distinct facial features of historical figures like Albert Einstein and General Leslie Groves, further immersing viewers in the film's world.

Hairstylist Shane Thomas played a vital role in completing the transformations. He meticulously researched period-specific hairstyles, ensuring each character's look accurately reflected their social standing and evolving personalities. Oppenheimer's hairstyle, initially youthful and neat, evolves to mirror his inner turmoil and the weight of his decisions.

The true genius of the makeup and hairstyling in "Oppenheimer" lies in its ability to go beyond mere visual transformation. The subtle changes in appearance reflect the characters' inner journeys and the emotional toll of living through a momentous historical period. Oppenheimer's increasingly tired eyes and disheveled hair visually communicate his growing disillusionment and ethical struggles.

The nomination for Best Makeup and Hairstyling is a testament to the dedication and artistry of Nelson, Thomas, and Vernon. Their meticulous attention to detail, deep understanding of the characters, and skillful application of their craft have resulted in a visually stunning and emotionally resonant portrayal of a complex historical narrative.

"Poor Things"

Yorgos Lanthimos' darkly comedic film "Poor Things" earned a well-deserved nomination for Best Makeup and Hairstyling at the 2024 Academy Awards, thanks to the exceptional work of makeup and hairstylist Nadia Stacey.

The film, based on Alasdair Gray's novel of the same name, tells the fantastical story of a young woman brought back to life using unorthodox methods and her subsequent adventures across continents. Stacey's creative and meticulous approach played a crucial role in bringing this whimsical world to life, capturing the film's unique blend of historical setting,

The film's protagonist, Bella Baxter (played by Emma Stone), is a unique character with the head of a beautiful young woman but the body of a Frankenstein's monster. Stacey created a custom prosthetic suit for this character, ensuring it was both visually striking and believable within the film's world. The suit itself was a marvel of design, featuring intricate stitching, realistic skin tones, and subtle imperfections that added to its believability.

Stacey's artistry went beyond simply creating the prosthetic suit. She used makeup and hair to further define Bella's character and her journey of self-discovery. Bella's makeup is often playful and whimsical, reflecting her childlike innocence and curiosity.

As the film progresses and Bella matures, her makeup becomes more sophisticated, mirroring her evolving understanding of the world and her own identity.

Hairstyle also played a significant role in shaping Bella's character. Her hair is initially kept short and messy, reflecting her wild and untamed nature. As she gains confidence and independence, her hair is styled in more elaborate and feminine ways. This subtle shift in hairstyle visually communicates Bella's transformation and her newfound sense of self.

Stacey's nomination for Best Makeup and Hairstyling is a well-deserved recognition of her creativity, skill, and understanding of the film's unique vision.

Her work not only contributed to the film's visual impact but also played a crucial role in shaping the character of Bella Baxter and conveying her emotional journey.

With "Poor Things," Stacey has delivered a masterclass in makeup and hairstyling, creating a character that is both visually stunning and emotionally resonant.

"Society of the Snow"

The Spanish film "Society of the Snow," based on the true story of two Uruguayan rugby players stranded in the Andes mountains after a plane crash in 1972, garnered critical acclaim for its harrowing portrayal of survival and resilience. Adding to the film's immersive and realistic experience was the exceptional work of the makeup and hairstyling team, led by Ana López-Puigcerver, Belén López-Puigcerver, David Martí, and Montse Ribé.

Their nomination for Best Makeup and Hairstyling at the 2024 Academy Awards is a testament to their dedication and artistry in transforming the actors into their real-life counterparts, weathered and desperate after 72 days in the harsh mountain environment.

The cast of "Society of the Snow" underwent a remarkable physical transformation to embody the survivors' ordeal. The makeup and hairstyling team meticulously recreated the effects of prolonged exposure to the elements, including extreme weight loss, frostbite, sunburn, and the growth of beards and hair. Prosthetic makeup was used to create realistic injuries and scars, further immersing the audience in the characters' physical struggles.

Hairstyling played a crucial role in conveying the emotional journey of the survivors. As the film progresses, their once-neat haircuts become increasingly overgrown and matted, reflecting their descent into desperation and despair. The subtle changes in hairstyles not only added to the film's realism but also served as a visual reminder of the passage of time and the toll it took on the characters' mental and physical well-being.

The success of the makeup and hairstyling in "Society of the Snow" lies in the seamless collaboration between the team members.

Ana López-Puigcerver and Belén López-Puigcerver's expertise in makeup, combined with David Martí's skill in prosthetics and Montse Ribé's talent for hairstyling, resulted in a cohesive and believable portrayal of the survivors' physical transformation. Their meticulous attention to detail and close collaboration with the actors ensured that the makeup and hairstyling served not only as visual effects but also as powerful storytelling tools.

The nomination for Best Makeup and Hairstyling is a well-deserved recognition of the exceptional artistry and dedication of the team behind "Society of the Snow." Their work played a crucial role in transporting audiences to the Andes mountains and immersing them in the harrowing experience of the survivors. By seamlessly blending historical accuracy with emotional resonance, the makeup and hairstyling elevated the film's narrative and contributed to its overall success.

Best Live Action Short Film

"The After"

In the realm of 2024 Academy Award nominees for Best Live Action Short Film, "The After," directed by Misan Harriman, stands out with its poignant portrayal of grief and healing. The film delves into the aftermath of a young woman's death, following her partner as he navigates the complexities of loss and attempts to find solace in their shared memories.

"The After" unfolds through the eyes of Kai (played by Joshua Oddie), who grapples with the sudden passing of his girlfriend, Elena (played by Gugu Mbatha-Raw). The film delicately explores the raw emotions of grief, showcasing Kai's struggle to come to terms with his reality and the void left by Elena's absence.

Director Harriman employs intimate handheld camerawork and close-up shots, bringing the audience closer to Kai's emotional turmoil and immersing them in his journey.

The film masterfully utilizes flashbacks to weave Elena's vibrant presence into the narrative. These glimpses of their shared past, filled with laughter and love, create a stark contrast to Kai's present loneliness. This interplay between past and present underscores the depth of their connection and the enduring impact of Elena's memory on Kai's life.

As Kai navigates his grief, he encounters Sarah (played by Janet Dacal), a woman who also carries the burden of loss. Their shared experiences create a bond of understanding and offer a glimmer of hope for healing. The film explores the power of human connection in overcoming grief, suggesting that finding solace can often be found in shared vulnerability and empathy.

The emotional core of "The After" rests on the powerful performance of Joshua Oddie as Kai. His nuanced portrayal captures the rawness of grief, the confusion, the anger, and the moments of quiet contemplation. Oddie's ability to convey these complex emotions without melodrama makes Kai's journey deeply relatable and resonates with the audience on a profound level.

With its delicate handling of a universal theme, its masterful use of cinematic techniques, and its moving performance, "The After" has earned its place among the nominees for Best Live Action Short Film. The film offers a poignant exploration of grief and healing, reminding us of the enduring power of love and the importance of human connection in overcoming loss.

"Invincible"

Among the captivating contenders for the 2024 Academy Awards Best Live Action Short Film stands "Invincible," directed by Vincent René-Lortie. This poignant Canadian film delves into the heart of a struggling family, weaving a tapestry of resilience, acceptance, and the extraordinary resilience of the human spirit.

The film centers around Michel (Rémi Goulet), a single father fiercely devoted to his teenage son Simon (Simon Pigeon), who suffers from Duchenne muscular dystrophy.

Despite overwhelming challenges, Michel remains a pillar of unwavering optimism and humor, providing his son with an environment of love and joy despite their difficult circumstances.

As Simon's condition worsens, the film paints a realistic portrayal of the emotional toll it takes on both father and son. The audience witnesses their moments of fear, frustration, and vulnerability, yet, the film never succumbs to sentimentality. Instead, it emphasizes the beauty of their unwavering bond, showcasing the strength they find in each other and their shared moments of laughter and light.

"Invincible" transcends the mere depiction of physical limitations. It celebrates the triumph of the human spirit, highlighting Simon's determination to live life to the fullest. Whether it's his passion for basketball or his mischievous pranks, the film emphasizes his zest for life, reminding us that joy and humor can bloom even in the face of adversity.

The film's success hinges on its powerful storytelling and moving performances. Director René-Lortie masterfully uses subtle yet impactful visual cues to convey the emotional depth of the narrative. The tender relationship between Michel and Simon is brought to life by the exceptional performances of Rémi Goulet and Simon Pigeon. Their genuine portrayal of love, pain, and resilience resonates deeply with the audience.

"Invincible" is a heartwarming and emotionally resonant film that offers a refreshing perspective on disability and family dynamics. With its poignant story, masterful execution, and exceptional performances, it's no surprise that the film has earned its place among the nominees for Best Live Action Short Film. It serves as a reminder of the unwavering strength of the human spirit and the transformative power of love in the face of adversity.

"Knight of Fortune"

The film centers around Karl (Leif Andrée), an elderly widower grappling with the recent loss of his wife. Lost in his sorrow and struggling to face the future, he encounters Torben (Oliver Due), another elderly man with his own burdens. Their chance encounter during a mundane errand sets in motion a series of interactions that unexpectedly change both their lives.

Despite their initial awkwardness, Karl and Torben discover a common ground in their shared experiences of loss and loneliness. Over cups of coffee and conversations laden with humor and vulnerability, they begin to find solace in each other's company. As they open up about their pasts and present struggles, a genuine connection forms, offering them a much-needed sense of understanding and support.

"Knight of Fortune" celebrates the transformative power of human connection.

In a world often focused on individual journeys, the film reminds us of the beauty and significance of finding unexpected companionship. Through Karl and Torben's interactions, the film highlights how simple acts of kindness and shared experiences can alleviate even the deepest grief and loneliness.

The film's success hinges on the remarkable performances of Leif Andrée and Oliver Due. Their portrayal of the two elderly men is filled with authenticity and warmth, allowing viewers to connect with their emotions and journey. Director Lasse Lyskjær Noer's delicate touch in navigating the narrative further elevates the film, capturing the subtle nuances of human interaction and the quiet moments of shared understanding.

"Knight of Fortune" is a poignant and uplifting film that leaves a lasting impression. Its message of hope, resilience, and the transformative power of human connection resonates deeply with audiences of all ages. With its exceptional storytelling, nuanced performances, and heartwarming message, the film's nomination for Best Live Action Short Film is a well-deserved recognition of its artistic merit and emotional impact.

"Red, White and Blue"

Among the captivating contenders for the 2024 Academy Award for Best Live Action Short Film stands "Red, White and Blue," directed by Nazrin Choudhury and Sara McFarlane. This visually stunning and emotionally resonant film delves into the complexities of identity and belonging, weaving a tapestry of experiences against the backdrop of a multicultural America.

The film unfolds through the interconnected stories of three women: Rosa (Luz Adriana Jiménez), a Mexican grandmother grappling with assimilation; Meena (Sonal Shah), a South Asian lawyer facing cultural expectations; and Jenna (Lovie Simone), a young Black woman navigating societal perceptions. Despite their diverse backgrounds, they share a common thread: the struggle to reconcile their individual identities with the expectations placed upon them by their families, communities, and the nation at large.

"Red, White and Blue" masterfully utilizes color symbolism to visually represent the internal conflicts and journeys of its characters. The titular red, white, and blue evoke the American flag, a symbol of unity and patriotism, yet the film explores the complexities and limitations of this singular narrative. Through nuanced cinematography and costume design, the film delves into the spectrum of emotions associated with national identity, showcasing both its unifying power and its potential to restrict and exclude.

Rosa, Meena, and Jenna embark on unique journeys of self-discovery as they challenge societal norms and redefine their relationships with their heritage and cultural expectations. Rosa embraces her cultural roots with renewed pride, Meena breaks free from traditional constraints, and Jenna asserts her individuality while acknowledging the weight of her history. Their personal transformations resonate with audiences, offering a message of empowerment and the importance of embracing one's authentic self.

The film's success hinges on the powerful performances of Luz Adriana Jiménez, Sonal Shah, and Lovie Simone.

Each actress embodies their character with depth and nuance, conveying the complexities of their emotions and journeys. Their portrayals resonate with audiences of diverse backgrounds, sparking conversations about identity, belonging, and the ever-evolving landscape of American society.

"Red, White and Blue" is a timely and thought-provoking film that challenges viewers to examine their own assumptions about identity and belonging. With its poignant storytelling, striking visuals, and moving performances, it's no surprise that the film has earned its place among the nominees for Best Live Action Short Film. It serves as a powerful reminder that the American identity is multifaceted and ever-evolving, and that true belonging lies in embracing our unique tapestry of experiences and perspectives.

"The Wonderful Story of Henry Sugar"

Among the captivating contenders for the 2024 Academy Award for Best Live Action Short Film stands "The Wonderful Story of Henry Sugar," directed by Luke Forbes. This witty and visually stunning film blends historical fiction with magical realism, transporting us into the captivating world of a man seeking to cheat fate through the extraordinary power of Yoga.

Henry Sugar (Mark Rylance), a wealthy playboy with an insatiable appetite for risk, stumbles upon the legend of Imdad Khan, a renowned yogi capable of seeing without his eyes. Driven by a desire to gain an edge in gambling, Henry embarks on a quest to master this seemingly impossible feat.

The film masterfully blends historical settings with fantastical elements. Henry's journey to hone his yogic abilities takes him from opulent casinos to secluded mountain retreats, immersing us in the world of Eastern mysticism and self-discovery.

The film explores the power of belief and its potential to shape our realities, blurring the lines between myth and truth, ultimately questioning what it truly means to "see."

Mark Rylance delivers a captivating performance as Henry Sugar, imbuing him with a mischievous charm and a hint of desperation. His witty monologues and playful demeanor draw the audience into his world, making us both question and root for his audacious ambitions.

Visually, the film is a treat. Cinematographer Dick Pope paints each scene with a rich palette of colors and textures, transporting us to bustling casinos, serene mountaintops, and dimly lit opium dens. The blend of period detail and dreamlike imagery creates a captivating atmosphere that perfectly complements the film's whimsical narrative.

As Henry hones his "unseeing" abilities, his success at the gambling tables grows, bringing him both wealth and notoriety. However, the film subtly explores the consequences of relying on deception and manipulating fate.

The line between ambition and obsession blurs, leaving viewers to ponder the true cost of Henry's extraordinary gift.

"The Wonderful Story of Henry Sugar" is a delightful and thought-provoking film that blends humor, historical fantasy, and philosophical questions. With its captivating performances, stunning visuals, and intriguing narrative, it's no surprise that the film has earned its place among the nominees for Best Live Action Short Film. It serves as a reminder that the pursuit of extraordinary abilities often comes with unforeseen consequences, leaving us to ponder the meaning of true vision and the path less traveled.

Best Animated Short Film

"Letter to a Pig"

In the realm of the 2024 Academy Award nominees for Best Animated Short Film,"Letter to a Pig" by

Tal Kantor and Amit R. Gicelter stands out with its powerful blend of emotional depth, captivating animation, and a poignant message advocating for animal rights.

The film unfolds through the eyes of young Lily, who writes a heartfelt letter to a pig named Oscar, destined for slaughter. Through her innocent but insightful reflections, the film delves into the ethical treatment of animals and the disconnect between our daily lives and the realities of factory farming.

The film's animation style is deceptively simple yet highly effective. Utilizing a minimalist watercolor aesthetic, it creates a dreamlike atmosphere that emphasizes the emotional core of the story. Soft colors and expressive character designs evoke empathy and draw viewers deeper into Lily's world and her connection to Oscar.

Music and sound design play a crucial role in elevating the film's emotional impact. The original score by Yoav Dahan beautifully complements the visuals, adding layers of melancholy and hope. The carefully crafted sound design immerses viewers in the sights and sounds of the farm, further highlighting the stark contrast between the idyllic world Lily imagines and the harsh realities faced by animals.

While rooted in Lily's personal connection to Oscar, the film's message transcends a single story. It challenges viewers to confront their own relationship with animals and question the ethics of factory farming practices. Ultimately, "Letter to a Pig" is a heartfelt plea for empathy and understanding, urging us to reconsider our treatment of creatures often seen as mere commodities.

With its poignant theme, evocative animation, and powerful emotional resonance, "Letter to a Pig" has earned its place among the nominees for Best Animated Short Film. The film's ability to spark important conversations and challenge viewers' perspectives makes it a contender with lasting impact.

"Ninety-Five Senses"

"Ninety-Five Senses": A Whimsical Exploration of Human Connection in the 2024 Animated Short Film Nominees

Among the captivating contenders for the 2024 Academy Award for Best Animated Short Film stands "Ninety-Five Senses," a delightful and whimsical stop-motion animation by husband-and-wife duo Jared and Jerusha Hess. The film transports viewers to a vibrant world where a quirky inventor seeks to expand human perception through his fantastical "Sensory Expansion Chamber," offering a humorous and heartwarming exploration of connection and the beauty of human experience.

In the quaint town of Willoughby, inventor Alexander Turnover (voiced by Nicholas Cage) dedicates his life to creating contraptions that enhance the human senses.

His latest invention, the "Sensory Expansion Chamber," promises to unlock 95 additional senses beyond the traditional five, a prospect that both excites and unnerves the towns people.

"Ninety-Five Senses" utilizes stop-motion animation with captivating charm. The meticulously crafted sets and characters, reminiscent of Tim Burton's whimsical style, draw viewers into Alexander's eccentric world. The animation breathes life into the quirky townspeople and their exaggerated expressions, perfectly complementing the film's humorous tone and playful narrative.

While Alexander's invention initially creates chaos and confusion, it ultimately becomes a catalyst for deeper connection within the community. As characters experience the world through new senses, they gain unexpected insights into themselves and each other. The film celebrates the unique qualities of each individual and emphasizes the importance of understanding and empathy in human relationships.

The film's humor stems from its witty dialogue, slapstick situations, and the sheer absurdity of Alexander's inventions. However, beneath the surface lies a heartwarming message about embracing individuality, overcoming fear of the unknown, and finding beauty in the ordinary.

With its blend of whimsical animation, quirky characters, and a message of inclusivity and connection, "Ninety-Five Senses" has earned its place among the nominees for Best Animated Short Film. The film's ability to entertain, provoke thought, and leave viewers with a smile makes it a worthy contender for the prestigious award.

"Our Uniform"

Standing out among the nominees for the 2024 Academy Award for Best Animated Short Film is "Our Uniform," a thought-provoking and visually stunning animation by Yegane Moghaddam.

The film takes viewers on a captivating journey into a world of enforced uniformity, where individuality is suppressed and self-expression is forbidden. Through its powerful imagery and subtle storytelling, "Our Uniform" compels us to question the cost of conformity and the importance of standing true to oneself.

The film unfolds in a monochromatic world devoid of color and vibrancy. Buildings are identical, clothes are unvaried, and citizens move in synchronized steps, adhering to a rigid social order. Every aspect of life is dictated by "the System," leaving no room for personal expression or deviation from the norm.

The film disrupts this sterile world with the arrival of a young girl dressed in a vibrant red uniform. Her unexpected appearance throws the town into disarray, sparking curiosity and questioning among the citizens. As curiosity turns to admiration, and then to a collective desire for change, the film explores the power of individuality to challenge established norms and inspire rebellion.

"Our Uniform" relies heavily on its striking visuals to convey its message. The stark contrast between the monochromatic world and the vibrant red uniform is symbolic of the struggle between conformity and individuality. The animation style is minimalistic yet expressive, focusing on the characters' gestures and facial expressions to communicate their emotions and inner conflicts.

The limited use of dialogue further emphasizes the power of visual storytelling and allows the audience to interpret the narrative through their own lens.

While set in a fantastical world, "Our Uniform" resonates with viewers across cultures and generations. The film prompts us to reflect on the pressures to conform in our own societies, the fear of standing out, and the importance of embracing our unique identities.

With its thought-provoking story, stunning visuals, and powerful message, "Our Uniform" has earned its place among the nominees for Best Animated Short Film. The film's ability to spark important conversations and challenge viewers' perspectives makes it a contender with lasting impact.

"Pachyderme"

Amongst the nominees for the 2024 Academy Award for Best Animated Short Film stands "Pachyderme," a haunting and beautifully crafted animated tale by Stéphanie Clément. The film delves into the memories of Louise, a young girl

spending the summer at her grandparents' home in the countryside. As the idyllic vacation takes a chilling turn, Louise finds herself confronting a long-buried family secret and the enduring power of the past.

The film utilizes a unique animation style, blending traditional hand-drawn techniques with digital elements. This creates a dreamlike atmosphere, blurring the lines between reality and memory.

Louise's childhood experiences are depicted with vibrant colors and playful imagery, while darker memories manifest as cracks in the ice, representing the trauma resurfacing from beneath the surface.

As Louise explores the forbidden areas of her grandparents' property, she stumbles upon unsettling clues hinting at a tragic event in her family's past. The animation shifts with her discoveries, becoming darker and more ominous, reflecting the emotional weight of her findings. The chilling presence of "Pachyderme," a monstrous entity lurking in the woods, serves as a symbol of the family's dark secret and the fear Louise must confront.

While the animation carries much of the narrative weight, the film masterfully utilizes sound design and music to enhance the emotional impact. The sparse dialogue reinforces the introspective nature of the story, allowing viewers to interpret Louise's internal struggles through her expressions and the evocative soundscape. The music underscores the building tension and the unsettling nature of the discoveries, further immersing the audience in Louise's journey.

"Pachyderme" transcends its specific narrative to explore universal themes of confronting trauma and the burden of family secrets. Louise's journey of uncovering the truth resonates with anyone who has grappled with their past and the courage it takes to face difficult realities. The film's subtle yet powerful exploration of these themes makes it a thought-provoking and emotionally resonant experience.

With its unique animation style, haunting atmosphere, and poignant exploration of human resilience, "Pachyderme" has earned its place among the nominees for Best Animated Short Film.

The film's ability to blend beauty and darkness, while offering a timeless message about facing our past, makes it a worthy contender for the prestigious award.

"War Is Over! Inspired by the Music of John & Yoko"

"War Is Over! Inspired by the Music of John & Yoko": A Dreamy Call for Peace Nominated for Best Animated Short Film

Among the powerful contenders for the 2024 Academy Award for Best Animated Short Film stands "War Is Over! Inspired by the Music of John & Yoko," a visually stunning and deeply moving animation by Dave Mullins and Brad Booker. The film utilizes the iconic anti-war message of John Lennon and Yoko Ono's music to create a dreamlike tapestry of hope and resilience, reminding us of the enduring power of peace activism and individual action.

The film unfolds in a soft, dreamlike world saturated with pastel colors and flowing lines. This visual style evokes a sense of childlike innocence and boundless imagination, perfectly complemented by the optimistic message of John and Yoko's music.

Characters move with graceful fluidity, symbolizing the interconnectedness of humanity and the potential for cooperation and collaboration.

"War Is Over!" weaves together fragments of John and Yoko's most recognized anti-war anthems, including "Give Peace a Chance," "Imagine," and "Happy Xmas (War Is Over)."

The musical selections seamlessly blend with the animation, creating a powerful emotional journey that underscores the film's core message of peace and unity.

While the film prominently features John and Yoko's music, the animation adds layers of depth and interpretation to their message. Images of doves soaring through the sky, children playing hand-in-hand, and communities rebuilding from destruction visually reinforce the ideals of peace, understanding, and collective action.

The film emphasizes the role of ordinary individuals in creating a more peaceful world. Simple acts of kindness, compassion, and collaboration are depicted as the seeds of positive change, reminding viewers that even small gestures can have a ripple effect. The animation style, with its focus on interconnectedness and flowing lines, further underscores the idea that we are all part of a greater whole and responsible for shaping our collective future.

With its dreamlike animation, powerful musical score, and timeless message of peace, "War Is Over! Inspired by the Music of John & Yoko" has earned its place among the nominees for Best Animated Short Film. The film's ability to evoke hope, inspire action, and remind us of our shared humanity makes it a contender with lasting impact.

Best Adapted Screenplay

"American Fiction" - Cord Jefferson

Cord Jefferson's "American Fiction," based on Percival Everett's novel "Erasure," has garnered a well-deserved nomination for Best Adapted Screenplay at the 2024 Academy Awards. The film masterfully navigates the treacherous waters of satire, offering a hilarious yet deeply insightful critique of the publishing industry's exploitation of Black storytelling and the enduring struggle for authentic representation in American popular culture.

The film follows Monk Ellison (Jeffrey Wright), a frustrated novelist and professor who feels stifled by the limitations placed on Black authors. To prove his point, he adopts the pen name "Ralph Ellison Van Leer" and writes a stereotypical, hyper-commercial "Black" novel filled with tired tropes and clichés. Predictably, the book becomes a runaway success, propelling Monk into the heart of a literary world he despises.

Adapting Everett's metafictional and satirical novel presented a significant challenge. Jefferson retains the core themes of racial representation and cultural appropriation, while also streamlining the narrative for the screen. The screenplay cleverly incorporates flashback sequences to delve deeper into Monk's past and motivations, adding emotional depth to his cynical persona.

The film's humor arises from its exaggerated yet recognizable portrayal of the publishing industry's obsession with formulaic "Black" narratives. The screenplay cleverly dissects the industry's exploitation of Black pain and trauma, while also poking fun at the self-serving agendas of literary gatekeepers and awards committees. However, beneath the surface of the satire lies a poignant commentary on the yearning for genuine representation and the frustration of being typecast and misunderstood.

The success of "American Fiction" hinges on its outstanding performances. Jeffrey Wright delivers a nuanced portrayal of Monk's inner conflict, capturing his anger, frustration, and ultimately, his yearning for artistic integrity.

Tracee Ellis Ross, Issa Rae, and Sterling K. Brown provide equally memorable performances as characters caught up in the whirlwind of Monk's satirical success.

With its sharp wit, insightful social commentary, and layered performances, "American Fiction" stands out as a masterful adaptation. The screenplay's ability to balance humor with poignant observations on race and representation makes it a worthy contender for the Best Adapted Screenplay award.

"Barbie" - Noah Baumbach, Greta Gerwig

Greta Gerwig and Noah Baumbach's audacious screenplay for "Barbie" has earned its place among the nominees for Best Adapted Screenplay at the 2024 Academy Awards. Their clever and subversive adaptation of the iconic Mattel doll transcends mere nostalgia, instead offering a witty and thought-provoking exploration of female identity, societal expectations, and the power of imagination.

The screenplay breaks free from the limitations of Barbie's traditional image, crafting a narrative that delves into the inner lives and aspirations of these plastic figures. Barbie (Margot Robbie), once content with her idyllic world of Dreamhouse perfection, finds herself questioning her purpose and yearning for a broader existence. The screenplay masterfully utilizes humor and metafiction to explore Barbie's existential crisis, challenging societal expectations and ingrained notions of femininity.

Gerwig and Baumbach's script seamlessly blends humor and philosophical insight. Barbie's journey takes her to the "real world," a land populated by humans who view her and her fellow dolls with amusement and confusion. This satirical juxtaposition allows the film to explore themes of conformity, the construction of beauty standards, and the challenges of self-discovery in a world obsessed with appearances.

While acknowledging Barbie's cultural significance, the screenplay avoids succumbing to mere nostalgia.

Instead, it reimagines the character and her world with a contemporary lens, addressing issues relevant to modern audiences. By weaving in pop culture references and metafictional elements, the script creates a playful and engaging narrative that resonates with viewers of all ages.

The success of "Barbie" hinges on its captivating performances. Margot Robbie shines as Barbie, delivering a layered portrayal of a woman grappling with self-doubt and existential confusion. Ryan Gosling's Ken is more than just a plastic counterpart, offering a surprisingly nuanced interpretation of masculinity and societal expectations. The supporting cast, including America Ferrera, Kate McKinnon, and Issa Rae, adds further depth and humor to the narrative.

"Barbie" stands out as a daring and inventive adaptation that defies expectations. Gerwig and Baumbach's witty screenplay offers a humorous yet insightful exploration of identity, societal pressures, and the power of imagination.

With its stellar performances and thought-provoking themes, the film earns its place among the contenders for Best Adapted Screenplay.

"Oppenheimer" - Christopher Nolan

Christopher Nolan's "Oppenheimer," based on Kai Bird and Martin Sherwin's Pulitzer Prize-winning biography "American Prometheus," has secured a well-deserved nomination for Best Adapted Screenplay at the 2024 Academy Awards. The film delves into the life and legacy of J. Robert Oppenheimer, the enigmatic "father of the atomic bomb," navigating the complex ethical and personal struggles surrounding the creation of this devastating weapon.

The screenplay moves beyond the historical figurehead, offering a nuanced portrait of Oppenheimer's brilliance, ambition, and moral ambiguity.

Nolan avoids hagiography or demonization, instead presenting Oppenheimer as a complex individual grappling with the immense weight of his scientific breakthrough and its potential consequences. The script explores his motivations, relationships, and internal conflicts, allowing viewers to form their own judgments about this controversial figure.

Nolan masterfully intertwines the personal and the historical, seamlessly blending scenes of Oppenheimer's scientific pursuits with intimate moments of his private life. This approach allows the film to explore the emotional and psychological impact of the Manhattan Project on those involved, adding a layer of depth and humanity to the historical narrative.

The film retains Nolan's signature visual style, employing grand visuals, innovative camerawork, and a driving sense of tension. However, these elements are carefully calibrated to serve the film's historical setting and emotional core. The script's tight pacing and suspenseful atmosphere keep the audience invested in Oppenheimer's journey, even as they grapple with the moral complexities of his work.

The success of "Oppenheimer" hinges on a powerful central performance. Cillian Murphy delivers a captivating portrayal of Oppenheimer, embodying his intellectual intensity, internal conflicts, and charismatic presence. Murphy's nuanced performance allows viewers to connect with Oppenheimer's humanity and understand the weight of his choices.

With its nuanced portrayal of J. Robert Oppenheimer, its exploration of the ethical complexities surrounding the atomic bomb, and its blend of historical accuracy and emotional resonance, "Oppenheimer" stands out as a remarkable cinematic achievement. Christopher Nolan's masterful screenplay earns its place among the nominees for Best Adapted Screenplay, reminding us of the power of storytelling to illuminate the lives and choices that shape history.

"Poor Things" - Tony McNamara

Tony McNamara's deliciously dark and audacious screenplay for "Poor Things," based on Alasdair Gray's novel of the same name, has garnered a well-deserved nomination for Best Adapted Screenplay at the 2024 Academy Awards. The film weaves a fantastical yet deeply human story about love, loss, and the complexities of identity, masterfully translating Gray's unique blend of satire and social commentary to the screen.

McNamara's adaptation takes the classic Frankenstein myth and injects it with a hefty dose of feminist critique. Bella Baxter (Emma Stone), a young woman reanimated with the brain of a drowned child, navigates a Victorian society obsessed with propriety and female subjugation. The screenplay cleverly utilizes Bella's monstrous nature as a metaphor for female empowerment, challenging societal norms and gender expectations with wit and subversive humor.

While the film gleefully pokes fun at Victorian attitudes and hypocrisy, it never loses sight of Bella's emotional journey. McNamara's script delves into her search for identity, her yearning for love and acceptance, and the challenges she faces as a creature deemed "unnatural" by society.

This balance between satire and heartfelt emotion allows the film to resonate with viewers on a deeper level, even as it entertains with its witty dialogue and outrageous situations.

The screenplay seamlessly blends historical accuracy with fantastical elements. Viewers are transported to the bustling streets of Victorian London, yet also encounter curious inventions and bizarre characters that heighten the film's comedic and satirical nature. This intricate tapestry of reality and fantasy allows for a unique exploration of Victorian society and its inherent contradictions.

The success of "Poor Things" hinges on its remarkable performances. Emma Stone delivers a captivating portrayal of Bella, capturing her innocence, vulnerability, and fierce determination. Mark Ruffalo shines as Dr. Godwin, the eccentric scientist who creates Bella, while Willem Dafoe offers a scene-stealing performance as the cunning and manipulative Odysseus. The supporting cast, including Olivia Colman and Terry Crews, further elevates the film with their quirky and memorable characters.

With its clever and subversive adaptation, its blend of satire and emotional depth, and its captivating performances, "Poor Things" stands out as a unique and memorable cinematic experience. Tony McNamara's masterful screenplay earns its place among the nominees for Best Adapted Screenplay, reminding us of the power of storytelling to challenge conventions and leave a lasting impression.

"The Zone of Interest" - Jonathan Glazer

Jonathan Glazer's disturbing and thought-provoking film "The Zone of Interest," based on Martin Amis' novel of the same name, has earned its place among the nominees for Best Adapted Screenplay at the 2024 Academy Awards. The film masterfully translates Amis' complex exploration of the Holocaust through the eyes of its perpetrators, offering a chilling and nuanced portrayal of evil's insidious nature and the blurred lines between complicity and responsibility.

The screenplay deviates from the traditional heroic narratives surrounding the Holocaust, instead focusing on the ordinary lives of those entangled in its machinery. We follow SS officer Rudolf Höss (Christian Friedel), the commandant of Auschwitz, as he builds a seemingly idyllic home for his family within the shadow of the death camp. The script delves into his banal routines, his domestic anxieties, and his interactions with other camp officials, showcasing the unsettling juxtaposition of everyday life and unimaginable horror.

Glazer's screenplay skillfully captures the fragmented and elliptical nature of Amis' novel. The narrative unfolds through a non-linear sequence of scenes, shifting perspectives and blurring the lines between reality and memory. This approach demands active engagement from the viewer, challenging them to piece together the complex moral implications of the characters' actions and choices.

The film confronts viewers with the uncomfortable reality of human complicity in evil. Through its portrayal of Höss and other characters who are neither monstrous villains nor heroic resisters, the screenplay forces us to consider the grey areas of moral responsibility and the ease with which ordinary individuals can be drawn into horrific acts.

"The Zone of Interest" features a captivating ensemble cast that brings the characters to life with unsettling realism. Christian Friedel delivers a chilling performance as Höss, capturing his banality and self-delusion with unsettling clarity. Sandra Hüller provides a counterpoint as his wife, Hedwig, her naivety and obliviousness serving as a stark contrast to the horrors surrounding them.

With its unsettling depiction of the Holocaust, its nuanced exploration of human complicity, and its masterfully crafted screenplay, "The Zone of Interest" stands out as a powerful and thought-provoking cinematic achievement. Jonathan Glazer's adaptation earns its place among the nominees for Best Adapted Screenplay, serving as a stark reminder of the enduring relevance and complexity of confronting historical atrocities.

Best Original Screenplay

"Anatomy of a Fall" - Justine Triet, Arthur Harari.

Justine Triet and Arthur Harari's chilling and enigmatic "Anatomy of a Fall" stands tall amongst the nominees for Best Original Screenplay at the 2024 Academy Awards. The film unfolds as a captivating courtroom drama intertwined with a complex personal tragedy, delving into the complexities of grief, suspicion, and the thin line between truth and fiction.

The screenplay begins with a devastating blow: the mysterious death of French author Adam Lassalle. His German wife, Nina (Sandra Hüller), becomes the prime suspect, thrust into a whirlwind of media scrutiny and legal battles. Through flashbacks and courtroom testimony, the narrative unravels the couple's turbulent relationship, riddled with secrets, misunderstandings, and unspoken resentments.

Triet and Harari's script masterfully utilizes language as a key driving force. Nina, a writer grappling with loss and cultural barriers, struggles to articulate her truth in a foreign language. The courtroom becomes a battleground of words and interpretations, where every carefully chosen phrase and nuanced expression holds the potential to twist the narrative and sway opinions.

"Anatomy of a Fall" transcends the confines of a traditional whodunit. The mystery surrounding Adam's death becomes a catalyst for exploring profound themes of grief, loss, and the burden of memory. Nina's journey through the legal system exposes the subjectivity of truth, the vulnerability of emotions, and the lasting impact of the past on our present.

The film's atmosphere is palpable, fueled by Triet's masterful direction and the evocative cinematography. Stark and haunting visuals complement the emotional complexity of the story, drawing viewers deeper into Nina's world of grief and confusion.

The performances, particularly Sandra Hüller's commanding portrayal of Nina, are nothing short of remarkable, adding layers of depth and nuance to the characters and their struggles.

With its intricately woven narrative, its exploration of language and its psychological depths, "Anatomy of a Fall" stands out as a truly original and engaging cinematic experience. Triet and Harari's masterful screenplay earns its place among the nominees for Best Original Screenplay, offering a profound and unsettling meditation on the complexities of human relationships and the elusive nature of truth.

"The Holdovers" - David Hemingson

David Hemingson's heartwarming and humorous "The Holdovers" has earned its place among the nominees for Best Original Screenplay at the 2024 Academy Awards. The film paints a captivating portrait of an unlikely bond forged between a strict classics teacher and a group of students forced to stay at their boarding school over Christmas break.

With its witty dialogue, poignant observations, and nostalgic atmosphere, "The Holdovers" offers a delightful blend of humor and heart.

The film opens during a snowy Christmas Eve, with a handful of students (Dominic Sessa, Oakes Fegley, and Alina Brace) stranded at the prestigious Elmwood Academy due to travel disruptions. Enter Mr. Clay (Paul Giamatti), a stoic classics teacher known for his rigid adherence to rules and his disdain for holiday cheer. Grudgingly tasked with chaperoning the students, Mr. Clay finds himself navigating unfamiliar territory: human connection and genuine joy.

Hemingson's screenplay masterfully peels back the layers of Mr. Clay's stern demeanor. As he interacts with the students, their youthful enthusiasm and genuine kindness chip away at his cynicism. Through witty exchanges, shared meals, and impromptu games, an unlikely friendship blossoms. Mr. Clay learns to embrace the spirit of the season, rediscovering the joys of human connection and the forgotten warmth within himself.

The students, too, embark on their own journeys of self-discovery. Hemingson's characters are far from one-dimensional; they each grapple with their own anxieties, aspirations, and family dynamics. As they spend time with Mr. Clay, they gain valuable lessons about resilience, empathy, and the importance of living in the present.

The film evokes a nostalgic atmosphere reminiscent of classic holiday movies, yet avoids feeling saccharine or predictable. Hemingson imbues the narrative with wit and contemporary social commentary, ensuring the story resonates with modern audiences. The setting of the prestigious boarding school adds a layer of intrigue and humor, highlighting the clash between tradition and individuality.

The talented cast brings Hemingson's characters to life with authenticity and charm. Paul Giamatti delivers a nuanced performance as Mr. Clay, capturing his initial grumpiness and gradual transformation with endearing humor. The young actors shine as well, each offering heartfelt and memorable portrayals of their characters' individual journeys.

With its witty dialogue, heartwarming premise, and relatable characters, "The Holdovers" stands out as a delightful and uplifting cinematic experience. David Hemingson's original screenplay earns its place among the nominees for Best Original Screenplay, reminding us of the power of human connection, the joys of unexpected friendships, and the importance of finding something to celebrate even in the most unexpected situations.

"Maestro" - Bradley Cooper, Josh Singer

Bradley Cooper and Josh Singer's deeply personal and ambitious "Maestro" has garnered a well-deserved nomination for Best Original Screenplay at the 2024 Academy Awards. The film delves into the tumultuous life and legendary career of composer Leonard Bernstein, weaving a tapestry of artistic passion, complex relationships, and the enduring power of music.

"Maestro" transcends the standard biopic format, offering a nuanced and introspective portrait of Bernstein's personal and professional struggles.

The screenplay delves into his volatile marriage to Felicia Montealegre (Carey Mulligan), exploring themes of love, ambition, and the sacrifices made for art. It also sheds light on Bernstein's struggles with his sexuality and identity, adding depth and complexity to his personal narrative.

Cooper and Singer utilize music as a powerful narrative device, mirroring Bernstein's emotional journey through iconic excerpts from his compositions. The audience experiences the triumphs and tribulations of his career alongside the soaring melodies and poignant harmonies of his music, creating a deeply immersive and emotionally resonant experience.

Not only does Cooper write and star as Bernstein, but he also makes his directorial debut with "Maestro." This dual role allows for a singular vision, seamlessly translating Bernstein's energy and passion onto the screen. The film's intimate camerawork and expressive visuals further draw viewers into the emotional core of the story.

Cooper delivers a tour-de-force performance as Bernstein, capturing his brilliance, his flaws, and his unwavering dedication to his art. Carey Mulligan shines as Felicia, embodying her strength, vulnerability, and complex relationship with her husband. The supporting cast, including Jeremy Strong and Maya Hawke, adds further depth and nuance to the narrative.

"Maestro" stands out as a powerful and poignant cinematic experience. The film's masterful original screenplay, its intimate portrayal of Leonard Bernstein, and its seamless integration of music and emotion make it a worthy contender for the Best Original Screenplay award.

"May December" - Samy Burch, Alex Mechanik

Samy Burch and Alex Mechanik's provocative and thought-provoking screenplay for "May December" has earned its place among the nominees for Best Original Screenplay at the 2024 Academy Awards.

The film delves into the scandalous true story of a teacher-student relationship that ignited a media frenzy and continues to spark discussions about age, power dynamics, and the complexities of love.

The screenplay avoids sensationalizing the headline-grabbing relationship between Grace (Natalie Portman), a charismatic English teacher, and Joe (Charles Melton), her 13-year-old student. Instead, it offers a nuanced portrayal of their emotional connection, exploring the factors that contribute to its formation and the lasting impact it has on both individuals.

Burch and Mechanik delve into the psychological motivations of both characters. Grace grapples with feelings of loneliness and dissatisfaction, seeking solace in the attention and admiration of her young student. Joe, yearning for validation and escape from a difficult home life, finds himself drawn to Grace's intelligence and affection. The screenplay avoids easy judgments, presenting a complex and layered understanding of their desires and vulnerabilities.

The film unfolds in a non-linear fashion, shifting between the present and past, as an actress (Elizabeth Olsen) prepares to portray Grace in a film. This approach allows for a deeper exploration of the long-term consequences of the relationship, showcasing how it shapes the course of both characters' lives and their perceptions of themselves and each other.

The film rests heavily on the shoulders of its talented cast. Natalie Portman delivers a mesmerizing performance as Grace, capturing her intelligence, vulnerability, and the internal conflict that arises from her actions. Charles Melton portrays Joe's journey with sensitivity and emotional nuance, highlighting the confusion and turmoil of adolescence. Elizabeth Olsen adds another layer of complexity as the actress grappling with the complexities of portraying Grace and understanding her motivations.

"May December" is not a film that shies away from difficult questions.

It challenges viewers to confront their own biases and consider the nuances of consent, power dynamics, and the long-term consequences of choices made in the heat of passion. The film's nomination is a testament to its ability to spark important conversations and provoke thoughtful reflection on challenging societal issues.

"Past Lives" - Celine Song

Celine Song's deeply moving and beautifully crafted "Past Lives" has garnered a well-deserved nomination for Best Original Screenplay at the 2024 Academy Awards. The film delves into the complexities of love, memory, and self-discovery, exploring the enduring impact of first love and the challenges of navigating cultural identity.

"Past Lives" transcends the traditional tropes of "first love" narratives. Song's screenplay offers a nuanced portrait of the relationship between Nora (Greta Lee) and Hae Sung (Teo Yoo), two childhood friends separated by the migration of Nora's family from South Korea to Canada.

Their emotional connection endures through years of distance, letters, and fleeting meetings, leaving an indelible mark on their lives.

The film weaves between past and present, seamlessly blending Nora's present-day life in New York with flashbacks to her childhood in South Korea. This structure allows for a deeper exploration of how memories shape identity and influence choices. Nora grapples with the weight of expectations, both cultural and personal, as she navigates her life in a new country while still yearning for her connection to Hae Sung and her Korean roots.

Song's screenplay sensitively explores the complexities of cultural identity and the challenges of belonging. Nora struggles to reconcile her Korean heritage with her American upbringing, constantly navigating cultural expectations and microaggressions. The film offers a nuanced portrayal of the immigrant experience, highlighting the challenges of assimilation and the longing for connection to one's roots.

The film's success hinges on its captivating performances. Greta Lee delivers a nuanced portrayal of Nora, capturing her inner conflict, emotional vulnerability, and quiet strength. Teo Yoo adds depth and tenderness to the role of Hae Sung, showcasing the enduring nature of their connection despite years of separation. John Magaro, as Nora's husband Arthur, offers a grounded and supportive presence that further highlights the complexities of her emotional journey.

"Past Lives" is a film that lingers long after the credits roll. Song's masterful screenplay delves into universal themes of love, loss, and identity with tenderness and insight. The film's poignant storytelling, its exploration of cultural complexities, and its captivating performances make it a worthy contender for the Best Original Screenplay award.

Best Supporting Actress

Emily Blunt, "Oppenheimer"

Emily Blunt has added another well-deserved accolade to her already impressive career with a nomination for Best Supporting Actress at the 2024 Academy Awards for her performance in Christopher Nolan's epic historical drama, "Oppenheimer." Stepping away from her usual leading lady roles, Blunt delivers a nuanced and powerful portrayal of Kitty Oppenheimer, the wife of the enigmatic "father of the atomic bomb," J. Robert Oppenheimer (played by Cillian Murphy).

Blunt, known for her action heroines and comedic timing in films like "Edge of Tomorrow" and "The Devil Wears Prada," showcases a different facet of her talent in "Oppenheimer." Kitty Oppenheimer is a complex and multifaceted character, grappling with the weight of her husband's scientific endeavors and the potential consequences of his work on the world stage.

Blunt's performance is subtle yet powerful, capturing Kitty's intelligence, strength, and unwavering support for her husband, even as she harbors doubts and anxieties about the project that defines his life.

While outwardly supportive, Kitty is not a one-dimensional character blindly following her husband's lead. Blunt masterfully portrays her internal conflict as she grapples with the moral implications of the atomic bomb. Her subtle expressions and nuanced dialogues reveal a woman who is both deeply affected by the ethical complexities surrounding the project and determined to stand by her husband, offering him emotional solace and unwavering loyalty.

"Oppenheimer" is a film that explores the vast scientific and historical implications of the atomic bomb. However, amidst the grand scale of the narrative, Blunt's portrayal of Kitty adds a crucial layer of humanity. Her character serves as an emotional anchor for the film, reminding viewers of the personal sacrifices and emotional turmoil that accompany monumental historical events.

Blunt's Kitty is not simply defined by her relationship to Oppenheimer. The screenplay, co-written by Christopher Nolan and his wife Emma Thomas, gives Kitty her own agency and voice. She stands up for her beliefs, expresses her concerns, and ultimately emerges as a woman of quiet strength and unwavering resolve.

Emily Blunt's performance in "Oppenheimer" is a testament to her versatility and talent. She seamlessly blends into the film's historical context while delivering a nuanced and emotionally resonant portrayal of a complex woman caught in the midst of history. Her nomination for Best Supporting Actress is a well-deserved recognition of her ability to elevate the film with her captivating presence and heartfelt performance.

Danielle Brooks, "The Color Purple"

Danielle Brooks has soared to new heights with her powerful and poignant performance in Blitz Bazawule's musical adaptation of Alice Walker's iconic novel, "The Color Purple." Her portrayal of Sofia, the fiercely independent and resilient spirit who defies oppression and embraces self-love, has earned her a well-deserved nomination for Best Supporting Actress at the 2024 Academy Awards. Brooks, best known for her Emmy-winning role as Taystee Chapman in "Orange is the New Black," brings a different type of strength and vulnerability to Sofia. Her character undergoes a transformative journey, escaping the clutches of abuse, finding her voice, and ultimately discovering the power of love and friendship. Brooks embodies Sofia's resilience with unwavering conviction, channeling her pain into courage and her anger into determination.

Sofia's journey is filled with moments of both resilience and vulnerability. Brooks navigates these emotional shifts with remarkable ease, capturing the raw pain of Sofia's experiences as well as the quiet moments of reflection and self-discovery. Her powerful vocals bring an added layer of depth to the character, allowing Sofia's emotions to soar through the film's unforgettable musical numbers.

Sofia's journey is not a solitary one. Brooks' chemistry with the film's other actresses, particularly Cynthia Erivo as Celie, creates a palpable sense of sisterhood and shared strength. Their bond offers hope and solace in the face of adversity, reminding audiences of the power of community and the unwavering support that women can find in each other.

While nominated for Best Supporting Actress, Brooks' role in "The Color Purple" carries the weight of the narrative alongside Erivo's Celie. Her journey is equally compelling, offering a different perspective on themes of oppression, self-discovery, and the fight for liberation.

"The Color Purple" is a story that resonates across generations, with themes of female empowerment and overcoming adversity remaining relevant. Brooks' performance embodies this timelessness, offering a contemporary interpretation of Sofia that speaks to both her generation and those who hold Alice Walker's novel close to their hearts.

With her nomination for Best Supporting Actress, Danielle Brooks has firmly established herself as a force to be reckoned with in Hollywood. Her talent, versatility, and commitment to portraying complex and powerful female characters make her a rising star with a promising future ahead.

America Ferrera, "Barbie" And Jodie Foster, "Nyad"

The 2024 Oscar nominations for Best Supporting Actress boast two captivating performances poised to steal the show: America Ferrera in Greta Gerwig's highly anticipated "Barbie" and Jodie Foster in the emotional biopic "Nyad."

Known for her comedic charm and relatable roles, Ferrera takes a bold step into the fantastical world of "Barbie." Details surrounding her character remain under wraps, but the sheer intrigue of seeing the talented actress navigate Gerwig's quirky and subversive take on the iconic doll has generated considerable buzz. Could she be a reimagined version of Barbie's best friend, Midge? Or perhaps a satirical nod to the unrealistic plastic perfection Barbie represents? With Ferrera's comedic timing and ability to embody complex characters, her "Barbie" role promises to be both hilarious and thought-provoking.

Jodie Foster, a seasoned veteran with two Oscars on her shelf, delivers a poignant performance in "Nyad." She portrays Diana Nyad, the real-life swimmer who made history by completing a solo swim from Cuba to Florida at the age of 64. Foster embodies Nyad's determination and resilience, capturing the physical and emotional challenges of the arduous feat with raw authenticity. Her portrayal goes beyond mere athleticism, delving into Nyad's personal motivations and the societal barriers she shattered with her incredible swim.

While their characters and films differ greatly, both Ferrera and Foster share a dedication to portraying multifaceted women who defy expectations. Ferrera's "Barbie" role promises to be a playful and enigmatic exploration of societal norms, while Foster's "Nyad" offers a powerful testament to human spirit and the audacity of dreams.

The Best Supporting Actress category this year is shaping up to be a fierce competition, and both Ferrera and Foster are strong contenders. Their diverse performances showcase the breadth of their talent and promise to be memorable additions to the awards season landscape. Whether they take home the golden statue or not, they have already garnered much-deserved acclaim for their captivating portrayals.

Da'Vine Joy Randolph, "The Holdovers

Da'Vine Joy Randolph has emerged as a frontrunner in the Best Supporting Actress race for her heartwarming performance in Alexander Payne's "The Holdovers." She breathes life into Miss Susie, a dedicated English teacher stranded at a prestigious boarding school over Christmas break with a handful of students. Her infectious spirit and unwavering optimism become a beacon of light during an unexpected holiday season.

Randolph, already a Tony Award nominee for her role in "Once on This Island," brings her undeniable stage presence and musicality to the film. Miss Susie's love for the arts fuels her passion for teaching, and Randolph flawlessly showcases this through impromptu carols and heartfelt renditions of classic poems. Her playful demeanor and genuine warmth quickly endear her to both students and viewers, creating a truly captivating character.

Miss Susie might be the life of the party, but Randolph imbues her with surprising depth. We see glimpses of loneliness and longing beneath her cheerful exterior, reminding us that even the most vibrant individuals have hidden vulnerabilities. This nuanced portrayal adds complexity and emotional resonance to Miss Susie, making her more than just a source of comic relief.

Randolph's comedic timing is undeniable. She delivers witty lines with impeccable comedic flair, often stealing the scene with her infectious laughter and playful gestures.

However, her comedic talent never overshadows her dramatic abilities. She seamlessly navigates Miss Susie's emotional journey, capturing moments of tenderness and vulnerability with heartfelt sincerity.

Da'Vine Joy Randolph's performance in "The Holdovers" is a breath of fresh air. Her captivating charm, infectious humor, and nuanced portrayal of Miss Susie have resonated with audiences and critics alike. Her nomination for Best Supporting Actress is a well-deserved recognition of her talent and a testament to her ability to steal hearts and awards season buzz.

Best Original Song

"The Fire Inside" from "Flamin' Hot"

The 2024 Oscar nominations sizzle with the inclusion of "The Fire Inside," the powerful ballad from Eva Longoria's biopic "Flamin' Hot." Written by Diane Warren and performed by Becky G, the song ignites the story of Richard Montanez, the man who invented Flamin' Hot Cheetos, capturing his passion, perseverance, and the fiery spirit that fueled his success.

"The Fire Inside" is more than just a catchy tune. Warren's lyrics delve into Montanez's journey, highlighting the challenges he faced as a Mexican-American janitor with a dream. Lines like "From mopping floors to burning bright, the fire inside wouldn't die" resonate with anyone who has ever dared to chase their dreams despite obstacles.

Latin music star Becky G brings the heat with her passionate vocals. She channels Montanez's determination and fiery spirit, injecting the song with raw emotion and undeniable charisma. Her dynamic performance perfectly complements the song's powerful message, making it an anthem for anyone who dares to dream big and defy expectations.

While "Flamin' Hot" tells the story of a spicy snack, "The Fire Inside" transcends the film's premise.

It becomes a universal anthem for overcoming adversity, embracing cultural identity, and pursuing your dreams with unwavering passion. The song's message resonates with audiences regardless of their background or personal struggles, making it a truly impactful addition to the Oscar race.

"The Fire Inside" stands out in the Best Original Song category with its blend of catchy melody, heartfelt lyrics, and a powerful performance by Becky G.

It's a song that stays with you long after the credits roll, reminding you to embrace your inner fire and fight for your dreams. Whether it takes home the golden statue or not, "The Fire Inside" has already earned its place as a scorching success and a contender to remember.

"I'm Just Ken" from "Barbie"

The 2024 Oscar nominations took a playful turn with the inclusion of "I'm Just Ken," the infectious pop anthem from Greta Gerwig's highly anticipated "Barbie." Performed by Ryan Gosling and a chorus of Kens (yes, you read that right), the song is a tongue-in-cheek exploration of masculinity, identity, and the perils of living in the shadow of a perfect plastic woman.

Gone are the days of Ken as Barbie's silent accessory. "I'm Just Ken" throws open the curtain on the inner lives of these impeccably groomed plastic men.

The song, penned by Mark Ronson and Andrew Wyatt, delves into their existential woes, questioning their purpose and yearning for individuality in a world obsessed with Barbie's perfection.

Ryan Gosling, known for his dramatic chops and comedic timing, takes center stage with a surprisingly soulful performance. He channels the collective voice of the Kens, their harmonies echoing the anxieties and aspirations bubbling beneath their perfectly coiffed exteriors. The song takes a humorous turn with its catchy chorus, "We may not have brains, but we have smiles / We may not have voices, but we sing for miles," delivered with playful irony by Gosling and his plastic posse.

"I'm Just Ken" doesn't shy away from social commentary. It playfully critiques societal expectations of masculinity, poking fun at the pressure men face to conform to unrealistic ideals of strength and stoicism. The song serves as a lighthearted yet thought-provoking commentary on gender roles and the quest for self-discovery, even for those molded from plastic.

Despite its playful premise, "I'm Just Ken" is unexpectedly catchy and well-crafted. The song boasts a vibrant pop melody, infectious harmonies, and witty lyrics that linger long after the last note fades. It's a song that will have you tapping your toes and questioning the meaning of being "perfect" in a world increasingly obsessed with appearances.

With its playful humor, catchy melody, and unexpected social commentary, "I'm Just Ken" stands out in the Best Original Song category. It's a song that entertains while prompting reflection, earning its place among the nominees with a wink and a nod to the power of pop music to tackle even the most plastic of issues.

"It Never Went Away" from "American Symphony"

The 2024 Oscar nominations resonated with a tender melody as "It Never Went Away" from Jon Batiste's "American Symphony" earned a well-deserved nod for Best Original Song. Written by Batiste and Co-penned by Dan Wilson, the song serves as a

poignant thread woven through the documentary, capturing the essence of resilience, love, and the enduring power of music in the face of adversity.

"It Never Went Away" began as a lullaby, a melody Batiste composed to offer solace to his wife, Suleika Jaouad, as she battled cancer. The song transcends its origins, transforming into a love song that celebrates their enduring bond and the strength they find in each other. Batiste's soulful vocals and the song's gentle piano melody create an atmosphere of intimacy and vulnerability, drawing listeners into their emotional journey.

While rooted in Batiste's personal experience, "It Never Went Away" expands beyond its origin story. The lyrics, "Through the darkest valleys, through the storms that rage, the melody remains, holding onto the page," resonate with anyone who has faced challenges and found solace in love, hope, and the unwavering human spirit.

The song's inclusion in "American Symphony" is particularly poignant. Throughout the documentary, Batiste grapples with composing a symphony that reflects the complexities of modern America. "It Never Went Away" serves as a reminder that music, in its simplest form, has the power to heal, connect, and offer solace amidst life's uncertainties.

In a world often filled with discord, "It Never Went Away" stands as a beacon of hope and harmony. Its simple melody and heartfelt lyrics offer a moment of respite, reminding us of the enduring power of love, music, and the human spirit to persevere. The song's nomination for Best Original Song is a testament to its emotional resonance and its ability to connect with audiences on a deeply personal level.

"Wahzhazhe (A Song For My People)" from "Killers of the Flower Moon"

The 2024 Oscar nominations resonated with a powerful voice from the past, as "Wahzhazhe (A Song for My People)" from Martin Scorsese's "Killers of the Flower Moon" earned a well-deserved nod for Best Original Song. Composed and performed by Oklahoman musician Scott George, the song serves as a poignant reminder of the resilience and enduring spirit of the Osage Nation amidst a period of historical injustice.

"Wahzhazhe" isn't merely a soundtrack addition; it's a living piece of Osage history woven into the film's narrative. The lyrics, sung in the Osage language, translate to "Osage Nation stand and be recognized," and "God made it for us." These powerful words echo through the film, serving as a rallying cry for the Osage people as they face the devastating reality of the Osage Reign of Terror.

George, an Osage Nation music consultant and composer, imbues the song with cultural authenticity. The traditional instrumentation, featuring hand drums and chanting, transports listeners to the heart of Osage culture. His vocals, imbued with both pain and defiance, capture the emotional depth of the Osage experience, reminding us of the human cost of historical injustices.

"Wahzhazhe" has transcended the boundaries of the film, becoming an anthem for the Osage Nation and a powerful statement on resilience in the face of adversity. The song's nomination marks a historic moment for Indigenous representation at the Oscars, recognizing the artistic value and cultural significance of Indigenous voices.

In a world often dominated by mainstream narratives, "Wahzhazhe" stands as a powerful reminder of the stories that remain untold. By giving voice to the Osage experience through music, George not only enriches the film but also sparks broader conversations about historical injustices and the importance of cultural preservation.

"Wahzhazhe (A Song for My People)" is not just a contender for Best Original Song; it's a testament to the enduring power of music to preserve history, ignite emotions, and empower marginalized communities. Its nomination represents a significant step towards greater inclusivity and recognition of diverse voices in the cinematic landscape.

"What Was I Made For?" from "Barbie"

The 2024 Oscar nominations took an unexpected turn with Greta Gerwig's "Barbie" landing a nod for Best Original Song with "What Was I Made For?". Performed by Ariana Grande, the introspective ballad delves into the seemingly perfect world of Barbie and questions the purpose and limitations placed upon her by societal expectations.

Gone are the days of Barbie as a silent fashion icon. "What Was I Made For?" cracks open the plastic facade, revealing a Barbie grappling with existential questions about her identity and place in the world.

Written by Billie Eilish and FINNEAS, the song's lyrics explore themes of self-discovery, societal pressures, and the yearning for more than just endless pink accessories and high heels.

Ariana Grande, known for her powerful vocals and introspective lyrics, lends her voice to Barbie's internal struggles. Her melancholic delivery captures the frustration and confusion simmering beneath the plastic smile, resonating with anyone who has ever felt confined by societal expectations or questioned their own purpose.

While the song tackles serious themes, it retains a playful edge that aligns with the film's subversive tone. The catchy melody and tongue-in-cheek lyrics, like "Made of plastic, heart elastic, was I built for sun and castles?" poke fun at Barbie's stereotypical image while raising thought-provoking questions about societal norms and gender roles.

"What Was I Made For?" is more than just a catchy pop song; it's a cultural commentary disguised in glitter and bubblegum pink.

It challenges the image of the perfect, passive Barbie and prompts audiences to consider the limitations placed upon women and the pressure to conform to unrealistic ideals.

With its introspective lyrics, playful rebellion, and Ariana Grande's captivating vocals, "What Was I Made For?" stands out in the Best Original Song category. It's a song that entertains while prompting reflection, earning its place among the nominees with a wink and a nod to the power of pop music to tackle even the most plastic of issues.

Best Original Score

"American Fiction"

The captivating melodies and evocative soundscapes of "American Fiction" have earned their well-deserved place among the nominees for Best Original Score at the 2024 Academy Awards. Composed by rising star Laura Karpman, the score seamlessly blends classical instrumentation with contemporary influences, reflecting the film's exploration of race, identity, and the fluidity of fiction.

Karpman eschews traditional orchestral bombast in favor of a more nuanced approach. Sparse piano melodies and hauntingly beautiful strings evoke a sense of longing and introspection, mirroring the internal struggles of the film's protagonist, Thelonious Ellison (Jeffrey Wright). Jazzy interludes infuse the score with a rhythmic energy, reflecting the vibrant culture and complex history of Black America.

The score masterfully bridges the gap between time periods, drawing inspiration from Ellison's literary influences like James Baldwin and Ralph Ellison. Hints of blues and African rhythms subtly weave through the orchestral textures, paying homage to the cultural roots of Black American expression. This fusion of past and present creates a cohesive sonic tapestry that reflects the film's exploration of identity and its evolution over time.

Karpman's score isn't simply background music; it acts as a vital narrative thread, heightening the emotional impact of each scene. Her poignant melodies perfectly capture the protagonist's moments of frustration, doubt, and ultimately, self-discovery. The music swells with hope and defiance during moments of empowerment, adding depth and complexity to the characters' emotional journeys.

"American Fiction" is more than just a collection of beautiful melodies; it's a carefully crafted sonic journey that reflects the film's themes and elevates its emotional resonance. Karpman's masterful blend of genres and influences creates a unique and captivating soundscape that lingers long after the credits roll. Her nomination for Best Original Score is a testament to her ability to use music to tell a story beyond words and paint a vibrant portrait of identity and its complexities.

"Indiana Jones and the Dial of Destiny"

The iconic fedora is back, and so is the composer who defined its cinematic adventures. John Williams' rousing score for "Indiana Jones and the Dial of Destiny" has received a well-deserved nomination for Best Original Score at the 2024 Academy Awards, marking a triumphant return for the legendary maestro.

Williams, at the helm of the "Indiana Jones" musical universe since 1981, understands the essence of the hero's spirit. His score for "Dial of Destiny" expertly blends nostalgia with thrilling new themes, rekindling the adventurous spirit of the franchise while offering fresh orchestral flourishes. Familiar motifs like the "Raiders March" soar through the score, instantly transporting audiences back to dusty tombs and daring escapes.

While honoring the film's legacy, Williams isn't simply retreading old ground. He introduces new thematic material that reflects the evolution of Indy and the film's contemporary setting. Broader orchestral textures and intricate percussion sections hint at epic new challenges and thrilling mysteries waiting to be unraveled. The score seamlessly merges the familiar with the innovative, ensuring both longtime fans and newcomers feel swept away by the adventure.

Williams, a master of cinematic storytelling through music, uses his score to heighten the film's emotional impact. Tense, suspenseful strings build anticipation during chase sequences, while triumphant brass fanfares celebrate Indy's victories. His music expertly guides the audience's emotions, immersing them fully in the film's action and peril.

"Indiana Jones and the Dial of Destiny" wouldn't be the same without John Williams' iconic score. His music is an integral part of the film's identity, weaving its own thrilling narrative alongside the on-screen action. His nomination for Best Original Score is a recognition of his enduring legacy and his ability to create music that defines cinematic adventure.

With Williams back at the helm, "Indiana Jones and the Dial of Destiny" promises an unforgettable sonic experience, proving that even after decades, the spirit of adventure still resonates through his timeless melodies.

"Killers of the Flower Moon"

Martin Scorsese's "Killers of the Flower Moon," a poignant exploration of greed and injustice within the Osage Nation, isn't just visually stunning; it's sonically captivating thanks to the masterful score by the late, legendary composer Robbie Robertson. Nominated for Best Original Score at the 2024 Academy Awards, this posthumous recognition celebrates Robertson's final musical journey.

Robertson, drawing upon his own Indigenous heritage and musical influences, crafts a score that resonates with both historical authenticity and emotional depth. Native American melodies and instrumentation intertwine with traditional orchestral elements, creating a soundscape that reflects the cultural heritage of the Osage people and the devastating impact of the oil barons' actions.

Somber violin passages and melancholic piano chords linger throughout the score, mirroring the pain and loss suffered by the Osage victims. Yet, moments of defiance and resilience shine through with stirring horns and driving percussion, echoing the spirit of resistance that kept the Osage Nation fighting for justice.

Robertson's score isn't simply a backdrop for the film's visuals; it actively drives the narrative forward. Specific themes are associated with characters and events, creating a deeper emotional connection with the audience. The haunting melody associated with the murders becomes a chilling foreshadowing, while the triumphant theme for Mollie Kyle (Lily Gladstone) underscores her unwavering determination.

Robbie Robertson's passing before the film's release adds a poignant layer to this Oscar nomination. It serves as a powerful testament to his artistry and his ability to translate historical injustice into a mesmerizing soundscape. His final work leaves a lasting impact, not just on "Killers of the Flower Moon," but on the world of film music as a whole.

With its ability to evoke historical echoes, emotional depth, and cultural authenticity, "Killers of the Flower Moon" stands out as a remarkable achievement in film scoring. This nomination, in essence, celebrates not just the technical brilliance of the score, but also the legacy of an extraordinary artist whose voice continues to resonate through his music.

"Oppenheimer"

The weight of history and the ticking clock of impending doom find their chilling counterpart in Ludwig Göransson's haunting and suspenseful score for Christopher Nolan's "Oppenheimer." Nominated for Best Original Score at the 2024 Academy Awards, Göransson masterfully captures the scientific ambition, moral complexities, and personal anxieties surrounding the creation of the atomic bomb.

Göransson eschews the typical Hollywood bombast of war films. Instead, he crafts a soundscape that pulsates with unease and uncertainty. Sparse piano melodies and distorted strings create a sense of paranoia and claustrophobia, mirroring the pressure and secrecy surrounding the Manhattan Project. Electronic textures hint at the untamed power of atomic energy, adding a layer of futuristic dread.

A recurring motif – a persistent, rhythmic ticking – becomes a constant reminder of the countdown to detonation and the immense responsibility borne by Oppenheimer and his team. This motif weaves in and out of the score, building tension and mirroring the ticking clock of fate that hangs over the film.

As the film progresses, and the ethical implications of the project become clearer, the score reflects Oppenheimer's growing internal conflict. Moments of soaring brass initially represent scientific discovery and national pride, but they gradually darken and distort, mirroring the moral gray areas surrounding the bomb's development.

Göransson's score isn't merely an accompaniment to the film's visuals; it serves as a vital narrative thread. The music viscerally conveys the emotional weight of the decisions being made, drawing the audience into Oppenheimer's internal struggle and the immense consequences of his actions.

"Oppenheimer" stands out as a unique and innovative addition to the world of film scoring. Göransson's masterful blend of traditional orchestral elements, electronic textures, and unconventional motifs creates a chilling soundscape that perfectly captures the complex themes and historical realities of the atomic age. His nomination for Best Original

Score is a well-deserved recognition of his ability to use music to tell a story that transcends words and leaves a lasting impact on the audience.

"Poor Things"

The Academy Awards have recognized the hauntingly beautiful and whimsical score of Yorgos Lanthimos' "Poor Things" with a nomination for Best Original Score.

Composer Jerkskin Fendrix weaves a sonic tapestry that perfectly complements the film's unique blend of Victorian satire, dark humor, and heartfelt emotion.

Fendrix eschews the typical orchestral flourishes often associated with period dramas. Instead, he crafts a unique soundscape that blends classical chamber music with modern electronica and playful flourishes. Delicate harpsichord melodies and melancholic cello solos evoke the Victorian setting, while quirky electronic interludes hint at the fantastical elements and Bella's unconventional existence.

The score masterfully reflects the emotional journey of Bella, the "unwoman" at the center of the narrative. Gentle string arrangements capture her initial innocence and wonder, while mournful woodwinds underscore her moments of loss and loneliness. As Bella experiences love and heartbreak, the music reflects her evolving emotions, with playful pizzicato strings hinting at her newfound independence and moments of triumphant brass celebrating her resilience.

"Poor Things" navigates between the stark realities of Victorian society and the whimsical world of Belle's creation. Fendrix masterfully mirrors this duality in the score. Somber piano chords and tense string sections paint a picture of societal constraints and prejudices, while whimsical woodwinds and playful percussion transport us to Bella's fantastical haven. This sonic contrast heightens the film's thematic exploration of societal norms and the yearning for acceptance.

Fendrix's score isn't simply a backdrop for the film's visuals; it actively drives the narrative forward. Specific themes are associated with characters and events, creating a deeper emotional connection with the audience. The melancholic melody associated with Bella's creator echoes his grief and longing, while the playful motif for Bella herself underscores her resilience and her quest for love and belonging.

"Poor Things" stands out as a captivating and innovative addition to the world of film music. Fendrix's bold blending of genres and his ability to translate the film's emotional core into an evocative soundscape make this score a remarkable achievement.

His nomination for Best Original Score is a well-deserved recognition of his artistry and his ability to create a unique sonic journey that lingers long after the credits roll.

THANKS FOR READING

Your opinion matters! Sharing your thoughts helps me grow as a writer and reach more readers like you. Plus, leave a review to get notified when Book 2 releases!

www.ingramcontent.com/pod-product-compliance
Lightning Source LLC
Chambersburg PA
CBHW071046290526
45795CB00004B/1343